THOUGHTS

OF

LOVE

Jacqueline Dodson

DEDICATION PAGE

THIS BOOK IT DEDICATED TO MY DADDY EXCELL LENARD WHO HAS
GONE HOME TO BE WITH THE LORD. HE BELIEVED IN ME AND LOVED
ME NO MATTER WHAT

TABLE OF CONTENTS

DISCLAIMER

SPECIAL THANKS

LOVE LETTER TO ME

I LOVE YOU DADDY

ALL THAT I DO

ANTHONY

BE TRUE TO YOU

CHOICES

DREAMING OF REMEMBERING LOVE

HAVE YOU

LOOKING BACK

OUR FIRST

PAIN AND HURT

LOVE LETTER TO ANTHONY AND TIFFANY

IS IT FAILURE

BEING WITH YOU

FOLLOW YOUR LEAD

GREAT TIMES

HAPPY 13TH BIRTHDAY TO MY SON

HOW COULD

HOW DID I GET HERE

I AM BLUE WITHOUT YOU

LIFE GOES ON

LONG DISTANCE LOVE

LOVING SOMEONE OTHER THAN ONE'S SELF

MY DAUGHTER TIFANY MY LOVE

OUR TIME

REFLECTING

TRUSTING

THINKING OF YOU

UNCERTAIN

UNHAPPY WOMAN

WHEN I AM TOSSED AND DRIVEN

WORDS CAN NOT EXPRESS

WRITING ON THE WALL

WOMAN OF EXCELLENCE

YOU ARE ALL THAT I WANT

YOU ARE RIGHT

YOU ARE FREE

YOU HAVE CAPTURED MY HEART

THERE IS NOT GOING TO BE

TABLE OF CONTENTS

DISCLAIMER

SPECIAL THANKS

LOVE LETTER TO ME

I LOVE YOU DADDY

ALL THAT I DO

ANTHONY

BE TRUE TO YOU

CHOICES

DREAMING OF REMEMBERING LOVE

HAVE YOU

LOOKING BACK

OUR FIRST

PAIN AND HURT

LOVE LETTER TO ANTHONY AND TIFFANY

IS IT FAILURE

BEING WITH YOU

FOLLOW YOUR LEAD

GREAT TIMES

HAPPY 13TH BIRTHDAY TO MY SON

HOW COULD

HOW DID I GET HERE

I AM BLUE WITHOUT YOU

LIFE GOES ON

LONG DISTANCE LOVE

LOVING SOMEONE OTHER THAN ONE'S SELF

MY DAUGHTER TIFANY MY LOVE

OUR TIME

REFLECTING

TRUSTING

THINKING OF YOU

UNCERTAIN

UNHAPPY WOMAN

WHEN I AM TOSSED AND DRIVEN

WORDS CAN NOT EXPRESS

WRITING ON THE WALL

WOMAN OF EXCELLENCE

YOU ARE ALL THAT I WANT

YOU ARE RIGHT

YOU ARE FREE

YOU HAVE CAPTURED MY HEART

THERE IS NOT GOING TO BE

IS IT LOVE

I LOVE YOU LORD

SPECIAL THANKS

TO MY CHILDREN ANTHONY AND TIFFANY WHO HAS SEEN ME IN THE BEST AND WORST OF TIMES AND I WILL ALWAYS BE GREATFUL. IT HAS NOT ALWAYS BEEN EASY YET WE LOVE EACH OTHER AND ARE THERE FOR EACH OTHER INSPITE OF OUR SHORT COMINGS WE LOVE EACH OTHER.......

GOD WHO HAS GIVEN ME ALL OF MY GIFTS AND SAW MY POTENTIAL BEFORE I EXSISTED. I LOVE AND THANK YOU ALWAYS

LOVE LETTER TO ME

YOU HAVE A PURE HEART AND I HONOR THAT ALSO THE DESIRE TO KNOW ME IN THESE LAST DAYS IS PLEASING TO ME. YOU HAVE A WAY ABOUT YOU THAT IS ROYAL AND PURE I HAVE LONGED FOR YOU TO COME TO ME, SEEK ME AND NOW THAT YOU HAVE JUST ASK ME WHATEVER IT IS, IT IS YOURS. I AM YOUR COMFORTER, YOUR PARTNER YOUR FRIEND, YOUR PROVIDER AND ALL THAT YOU WANT, NEED AND DESIRE IS AT HAND.

SO DO NOT FEAR OR WORRY ABOUT WHAT IS TO COME I AM HERE FOR YOU TODAY AND ALWAYS

I LOVE YOU MY DAUGHTER AND THAT IS FOREVER AND ALWAYS

YOUR FATHER IN HEAVEN

AMEN

I LOVE YOU DADDY

EVEN THOUGH THERE ARE TIMES WHEN YOU WERE NOT AROUND

MANY TIMES I WORE A FROWN

I LOVE YOU DADDY

I REALIZE THAT YOU LOVE ME

I HAD TO ALLOW THAT TO BECOME A REALITY

I LOVE YOU DADDY

I AM GLAD THAT WE SPEND TIME TOGETHER I HAVE MEMORIES THAT I WILL ALWAYS CHERISH YOU ALLOWED ME TO COME TO YOU TO TALK TO LAUGH AND CRY

YOU ARE MY DADDY AND I LOVE YOU I DO AND IT IS FOR REAL WE DO NOT HAVE TO TRY

I LOVE YOU DADDY

YOU ARE FIESTY LOVE SPORTS AND ARE STRONG

IN MY EYES YOU CAN DO NO WRONG

I LOVE YOU DADDY

YOU HAVE BEEN THERE FOR ME

I WANT YOU TO KNOW I WILL LOVE YOU FOR AN ETERNITY

I LOVE YOU DADDY

I AM GLAD YOU ARE IN MY LIFE

THERE IS NO STRIFE

I LOVE YOU DADDY

I MISS YOU BUT I REALIZE THAT YOU ARE NEAR

WITH THAT CONFIDENCE THERE IS NO FEAR

I LOVE YOU DADDY

YOU DO NOT LIKE TO HEAR ME CRY

KNOWING THAT I WILL TRY

ALL THAT I DO

ALL THAT I DO

I WANT TO BE PLEASING TO YOU

I CAN NOT COME OR GO UNLESS YOU SAY SO

I HAVE NO LIFE WITHOUT YOU

SO WHY MAKE MYSELF MISERABLE AND BLUE

I CAN NOT DO ANYTHING WITHOUT YOU

I KNOW THAT YOU ARE TRIED AND TRUE

EVEN WHEN I CAN NOT SEEM TO FIND MY WAY

YOU ARE WITH ME EACH AND EVERYDAY

TIMES GET TOUGH

YOU BRING ME OUT OF THINGS THAT ARE ROUGH

THERE IS NO ME WITHOUT YOU

WE ARE ONE I SAID YES I DO

THERE IS NO PROBLEM TO BIG OR SMALL

I PUT MY TRUST IN YOU AND I NEVER FALL

SOMETIMES WHEN I HEARD IT SPOKE

OFTEN TIMES I THOUGHT IT A JOKE

TRUST IN THINGS I CAN NOT SEE

WHEN MY LIFE WAS A MESS A REALITY

ONE DAY I HAD TO REALIZE

NO MATTER WHAT YOU ARE WISE

I COULD TRY TO FIX IT AND MAKE IT WORSE

OR TRUST AND BELIEVE AND PUT YOU FIRST

NO MATTER WHAT COMES MY WAY

THERE IS ALWAYS A BRIGHTER DAY

I LOVE YOU

ANTHONY

YOU ARE MY SON

AND I LOVE YOU A TON

YOU ARE MY FIRST BORN

YET I WAS NEVER TORN

I HAVE RAISED YOU TO BE STRONG WISE SMART AND TO DO WHAT IS RIGHT

MANY TIMES YOU PUT UP A FIGHT

THROUGH IT ALL I AM PROUD THAT YOU ARE MY SON

ALL IS WELL AND YOU ARE NOT DONE

I WANT YOU TO SHOW RESPONSIBILITY

SOMEHOW I BELIEVE THAT YOU NOW SEE

HOLD YOUR HEAD UP AND BE PROUD OF WHO YOU ARE

IN THIS LIFE THAT WILL TAKE YOU FAR

YOU HAVE A WARM SMILE FUNNY AND TALL

GO FORTH MAKE UP YOUR MIND AND YOU SHALL ACHIEVE ALL

BE TRUE TO YOU

WHEN YOU LOOK INSIDE DEEP INSIDE THERE IS A VOID

IF YOU CAN NOT BE HONEST WITH ANYONE ELSE BE TRUE TO YOU

YOU HAVE TRIED FILLING THAT VOID WITH MANY THINGS AND EVEN WITH PEOPLE

IF YOU CAN NOT BE HONEST WITH ANYONE ELSE BE TRUE TO YOU

WHEN YOU ARE ABLE TO LOOK IN THE MIRROR AND SEE THE REFLECTION STARING BACK AT YOU AND THERE IS SOMETHING MISSING

IF YOU CAN NOT BE HONEST WITH ANYONE ELSE BE TRUE TO YOU

WHEN YOU ARE ALL ALONE AND YOUR MIND IS RACING AND THERE IS NO PEACE WITHIN

IF YOU CAN NOT BE HONEST WITH ANYONE ELSE BE TRUE TO YOU

WHEN YOU ARE GOING THRU THE MOTIONS OF GETTING PAST THE SECOND, THE MINUTE, THE HOUR, THE DAY

IF YOU CAN NOT BE HONEST WITH ANYONE ELSE BE TRUE TO YOU

WHEN YOU WANT TO SCREAM OUT BUT NOT SURE WHERE TO START

IF YOU CAN NOT BE HONEST WITH ANYONE ELSE BE TRUE TO YOU

WHEN YOU REALLY LOOK DEEP INSIDE AND THERE IS A VOID AT SOME POINT KNOWING THAT YOU HAVE STRAYED AWAY FROM WHAT IS REACHING OUT TO YOU AND SUSTAINING YOU

IF YOU CAN NOT BE HONEST WITH ANYONE ELSE BE TRUE TO YOU

YOU REALIZE THAT THE SOURCE OF YOUR EXSISTENCE IS THERE AND WANTS TO SHOW YOU THE BEST YOU POSSIBLE

IF YOU CAN NOT BE HONEST WITH ANYONE ELSE BE TRUE TO YOU

ALLOW THE BEST YOU TO START BLOSSOMING INTO THE PERSON YOU ARE CREATED TO BE

IF YOU CAN NOT BE HONEST WITH ANYONE ELSE BE TRUE TO YOU

THERE ARE GOING TO BE BUMPS ALONG THE WAY BUT YOUR ASSURANCE IS THAT YOU ARE NOT ALONE

IF YOU CAN NOT BE HONEST WITH ANYONE ELSE BE TRUE TO YOU

WHEN YOU DEAL WITH THE DILEMAS AS THEY COME AND KEEP MOVING TOWARD THE BEST YOU

IF YOU CAN NOT BE HONEST WITH ANYONE ELSE BE TRUE TO YOU

ALWAYS NO MATTER WHAT COMES OR GOES OR WHO COMES AND GOES IN YOUR LIFE

IF YOU CAN NOT BE HONEST WITH ANYONE ELSE BE TRUE TO YOU

CHOICES

UP OR DOWN IN OR OUT LEFT OR RIGHT

CHOICES

HOWEVER WHEN THE CHOICES ARE SHE HER OR ME

WHEN YOU WANT TO WALK OR DRIVE UNDER THE MOON AND STARS WOULD IT BE SHE HER OR ME

CHOICES

WHEN YOU WANT TO SEND FLOWERS JUST BECAUSE WOULD IT BE SHE HER OR ME

CHOICES

WHEN YOU WANT TO BE SPONTANEOUS WOULD IT BE SHE HER OR ME

CHOICES

WHEN YOU WANT TO TAKE SOMEONE TO AND FROM WORK WOULD IT BE SHE HER OR ME

CHOICES

WHEN IT COMES DOWN TO IT IF YOU WANT SOMEONE TO BE WITH TO WINE AND DINE WOULD IT BE SHE HER OR ME

CHOICES

WHEN YOU WANT TO LOOK TOWARD THE FUTURE WOULD IT BE SHE HER OR ME

OBVIOUSLY IT IS NOT ME

CHOICES

WOULD IT BE GOOD TO PLEAD MY CASE AND LET YOU KNOW WHY IT SHOULD ME NOT HER OR SHE

CHOICES

WOULD IT BE GOOD TO REMEMBER AND CHERISH ALL THE GOOD
TIMES THAT WE HAD OR TRY TO FORGET THAT IT IS NOT ME BUT SHE
OR HER

CHOICES

WOULD IT BE GOOD FOR ME TO ROLL UP IN A BALL AND DIE OR
CHOOSE LIFE

I HAVE DECIDED MY CHOICE IS LIFE

DREAMING OF REMEMBERING LOVE

(THINGS ARE SO FOGGY YET THERE IS A SMALL CLEARING AND WHILE APPROACHING CAUTIOUSLY THERE IS SOMEWHAT OF CURIOSITY) THERE APPEARS TO BE TWO PEOPLE THAT ARE TOTALLY ENGROSSED WITH ONE ANOTHER. THEY ARE SO INTO EACH OTHER THAT NOTHING AROUND THEM SEEMS TO MATTER. THEY ARE EXTREMELY CONNECTED WITH EACH OTHER AS THEY SHARE WHAT SEEMS TO BE MANY MOMENTS OF ENCHANMENT. AS THEY DANCE TOGETHER UNDER THE MOONLIGHT AND STARRY SKY TO SUCH A BEAUTIFUL AND HARMONIOUS MELODY. (LEAVES HER BREATHLESS) TIME SEEMS TO STAND STILL FOR THEM ON A FALL NIGHT.

THE COUPLE ARE SO ONE WITH EACH OTHER. IT WOULD APPEAR THAT NOT ONCE DID THEY STOP LOOKING INTO EACH OTHERS EYES. (AT THIS POINT SOMETHING ABOUT THE WAY THEY LOOKED AT EACH OTHER THE WAY THAT THEY EMBRACED EACH OTHER WAS A SOMEWHAT FAMILIAR EXPRESSION. HOWEVER FAMILIAR SHE HAD TO BE VERY PRECISE BY TAKING THE NECESSARY PRECAUTIIONS. SHE APPEARS TO BE DREAMING. ALL THE WHILE MORE FOCUSED INTO WHAT SHE WAS EXPERIENCING AT THAT INTERVAL. SHE COULD NOT QUITE MAKE OUT THE WORDS OF EXPRESSION THE COUPLE WERE SAYING TO EACH OTHER. SHE TRIED TO IMAGINE THE COUPLE SAYING HOW MUCH THEY LOVED EACH OTHER, THAT THEY COULD NOT ASK FOR A BETTER MORE PERFECT PERSON TO SHARE THESE MOMENTS WITH. TO GET WHAT

THEY HAD WAS WHAT SHE NEEDED TO DO AT THIS POINT. SHE WANTED TO KNOW WITH CERTAINTY THAT THEY WERE INDEED EXPRESSING TRUE REFLECTIONS OF THOSE DEEP AND INTIMATE FEELINGS THAT CAME FROM DEEP WITHIN, NOT SUPERFICIAL. AS, THE HAZE IS CLEAR ENOUGH FOR HER TO MAKE OUT THE COUPLES SEEMINGLY AFFECTION, THAT APPEARS TO BE FAMILIAR TO HER. HOW COULD THIS BE?) THE COUPLE HAVE A DEEP PASSION AND RESPECT FOR ONE TO ANOTHER. THERE IS A GENTLE TOUCH OF HIS FACE AND DONE SO LOVINGLY AND WITH SUCH TENDER CARE. AT THAT MOMENT IT WAS CAPTURED WITH AN EVERLASTING HEART FELT MOMENT. THE

UNBRIDLED WAY HE TOUCHED HER HAND AS HE KISSED EACH ONE OF HER SOFT AND TENDER FINGERS WAS ENOUGH TO SEIZE ATTENTION.

(SHE CAUTIOUSLY APPROACHES AS HER HEART IS POUNDING VERY RAPIDLY. SHE IS NOW CLOSE ENOUGH TO SEE THAT SHE IS THE LADY THAT IS EXPERIENCING THE DREAMS OF REMEMBERING LOVE. HOW COULD THIS BE? FOR SO LONG SHE HAS SUPPRESSED THE MERE FEELING OF LOVE UNTIL SHE DID NOT KNOW IT WHEN SHE WAS FACED WITH THIS EMOTION. AFRAID TO EVEN DARE TO BELIEVE THAT THIS COULD ONE DAY BE HER. SHE WAS CONTENT IN HIDING HER FEELINGS FROM SUCH SENTIMENT. SOMEHOW, BLISS WAS SO FAR REMOVED. YET SHE IS REMEMBERING DREAMS OF LOVE. SHE FINALLY KNEW WHAT WAS SO COMMONPLACE ABOUT THE COUPLE. HOWEVER, NOT ONCE DID IT DAWN ON HER THAT SHE WOULD ONCE AGAIN OPEN HER HEART TO FEEL THE WONDERFUL LOVE AND DEVOTION THAT A MAN AND A WOMAN CAN EXPERIENCE IN THE PERFECT TIME.)

HAVE YOU

HAVE YOU EVER WANTED SOMETHING SO MUCH IT HURT TO IMAGINE YOURSELF WITHOUT IT

HAVE YOU EVER DREAMED OF BEING WITH SOMEONE WHO COMPLETED YOU

HAVE YOU EVER IMAGINED YOURSELF WALKING IN THE SAND ALONG SIDE WATER THAT WAS SO CAPTIVATING YOU COULD NOT IMAGE LOOKING AWAY

HAVE YOU EVER DREAMED OF BEING IN SOMEONE'S ARMS UNTIL HOLDING YOUR SELF BECAME A REALITY

HAVE YOU EVER LET SOMONE GO AND INTENSE PAIN CAME OVER YOU DOWN TO YOUR INNER MOST BEING

HAVE YOU EVER WANTED TO REACH OUT BUT YOU DID NOT KNOW WHAT YOU WERE REACHING OUT TO OR FOR

HAVE YOU EVER CRIED SO MUCH UNTIL THERE JUST WERE NOT ANY MORE TEARS PRESENT

HAVE YOU EVER TRIED TO PUT ONE FOOT IN FRONT OF THE OTHER YET COULD NOT MOVE

HAVE YOU EVER HELD YOUR PHONE SO TIGHTLY PRESSED TO YOUR CHEST UNTIL YOU FEEL ASLEEP HOPING THAT IT WOULD RING

HAVE YOU EVER GIVEN AWAY THE ONLY THING YOU HAVE EVER SOUGHT AFTER AND PREFERRED IN SUCH A LONG, LONG TIME

HAVE YOU EVER WAITED IN SILENCE THINKING AND RELIVING THE DECISION THAT WAS MADE AND WONDER WAS IT THE BEST CHOICE

HAVE YOU EVER KEPT YOURSELF BUSY TO AVOID FACING THE PAIN THAT IS FELT INSIDE

HAVE YOU EVER JUST SAID STAY STURDY FOCUSED AND IT IS GOING TO BE ALL RIGHT

HAVE YOU EVER DID A SELF CHECK AND BECOME CONSCIOUS TO THE ACTUALITY THAT WHAT YOU WERE SEEKING WAS NOT FOR YOU AT THAT POINT IN TIME AND YOU TRIED TO FIT A SQAURE PEG IN THE PLACE WHERE A CIRCLE PEG SHOULD FIT

IT JUST WAS NOT MEANT TO BE NO MATTER HOW HARD YOU TRY

HAVE YOU EVER SMILED OR LAUGHED AT YOURSELF FOR BEING SO OUT OF YOUR ELEMENT UNTIL EVEN YOU COULD DO NOTHING BUT PICK YOURSELF UP AND MOVE TOWARDS WHAT IS FOR YOU AT THE PRECISE TIME

WHEN YOU ARE AT THE PLACE YOU SHOULD BE THINGS COME TO YOU WITH SUCH EASE

LOOKING BACK

I REMEMBER THE DAY THAT I KNEW THAT I WOULD ALWAYS HAVE SOMEONE TO BOND WITH. IT WAS AN INSTANT CONNENCTION WITH HER AND I

LOOKING BACK

I REMEMBER THE PRICELESS VALUE THAT I HAD ESTABLISHED BETWEEN HER AND I THERE WOULD BE NOTHING THAT WOULD BE WITHHELD FROM HER. ONLY THE BEST FOR THE BEST

LOOKING BACK

THE DAYS TO COME WOULD ONLY BRING ME SUCH JOY AND DELIGHT. IN WORDS ELATED WOULD BE HARD TO DESCRIBE ONLY I FELT COMPLETE WITH HER IN MY LIFE A WELCOME ADDITION TO MY WORLD

LOOKING BACK

IT WOULD ALWAYS BE MY JOB TO KEEP HER FROM ALL MANNER OF HARM. TO KEEP HER SAFE IN MY ARMS IS ALL I WANTED TO DO.

LOOKING BACK

I HAD NO BOUNDARIES WHEN IT CAME TO HER THE WORLD WAS FOR HER IF SHE ASKED. MY THOUGHTS FOR HER WERE ALWAYS OF HOPE, PEACE, JOY AND TOTAL CONTENTMENT

LOOKING BACK

HOW COULD THINGS GO FROM JOY TO SADNESS IN WHAT SEEMS LIKE AN INSTANT

LOOKING BACK

I NEVER THOUGHT THAT ONE DAY I WOULD BE IN A PLACE OF UNCERTAINTY ABOUT HER. I CHERISHED HER VERY BEING WHEN I LOOKED INTO HER EYES I SAW THAT GOD HAD CREATED SOMEONE

PERFECT IN EVERY WAY

LOOKING BACK

DID I EVER IMAGINE THAT I WOULD LOSE SLEEP WITH NOT KNOWING WHEN, WHERE, OR HOW

LOOKING BACK

THAT IS ALL I WANT TO DO BECAUSE TRYING TO MOVE FORWARD HURTS DOWN TO THE INNER MOST PART OF MY SOUL

LOOKING BACK

THINGS WERE SAID AND ACTIONS WERE TAKEN BUT NEVER COULD I HAVE IMAGINED THAT WITHOUT HER MY LIFE WOULD BE SO EMPTY

LOOKING BACK

IS ALL I WANT TO DO BECAUSE TRYING TO MOVE FORWARD HURTS DOWN TO THE INNER MOST PART OF MY SOUL

LOOKING BACK

I NEVER IMAGINED THAT I WOULD NOT SEE HER EVERYDAY TO TAKE CARE OF HER AND TO KEEP HER SAFE FROM ALL MANNER OF HARM

LOOKING BACK

I S ALL I WANT TO DO BECAUSE TRYING TO MOVE FORWARD HURTS DOWN TO THE INNER MOST PART OF MY SOUL

LOOKING BACK

WHEN I FIRST SAW HER IT WAS LIKE LOOKING AT A PERFECT CREATION THAT I HAD ONLY KNOWN ONCE BEFORE IN MY LIFE

LOOKING BACK

I SOMETIMES WONDER WHY THINGS HAVE TO CHANGE BUT WITHOUT

CHANGE THERE CAN BE NO GROWTH, NO PROGESS, NO GETTING PAST THE HURT AND THE PAIN

LOOKING BACK

IS ALL I WANT TO DO BECAUSE TRYING TO MOVE FORWARS HURTS DOWN TO THE INNER MOST PART OF MY SOUL

YET TIFFANY NO MATTER WHAT WE GO THRU YOU ARE MY DAUGHTER AND MY LOVE FOR YOU NEVER ENDS.

OUR FIRST

I AM BIG ON FIRSTS LIKE

OUR FIRST MEETING OR ENCOUNTER

OUR FIRST DATE

OUR FIRST KISS

THE FIRST TIME WE LOOKED INTO EACH OTHERS EYES

THE FIRST TIME I KNEW I WANTED YOU IN MY LIFE ALWAYS

THE FIRST DISAGREEMENT AND THE FIRST MAKE UP

NOW WE EMBARK UPON OUR FIRST VALENTINE'S DAY TOGETHER

THIS DAY AND THE DAYS TO COME HOLD SUCH SIGNIFICANCE

I LOOK FORWARD TO MANY MORE FIRSTS WITH YOU BECAUSE YOU
BRIGHTEN UP MY DAY WITH YOUR SMILE AND YOUR LAUGHTER
INDICATE SO MUCH

WHEN MY DAY IS NOT GOING PROPERLY YOU LISTEN AND SAY THE
RIGHT THING TO HELP ME TO REFOCUS MY THOUGHTS

YOU ARE SPECIAL TO ME I WANT YOU AND I TO ASCEND TO HIGHER
HEIGHTS AND DEEPER DEPTHS TOGETHER

YOU ARE MY LOVE AND I DO NOT TAKE THAT FOR GRANTED

I CHERISH ALL THE TIME WE SPEND TOGETHER LONG AND SHORT

I LOOK FORWARD TO OUR EMBRACE IT FEELS GOOD WHEN WE ARE IN
EACH OTHERS ARMS

THERE ARE SO MANY THINGS THAT WE ARE GOING TO ENCOUNTER
TOGETHER GOOD, BAD, HAPPY OR SAD BUT WITH YOU I LOOK
FORWARD TO FACING ALL THINGS

PAIN AND HURT AND HURT AND PAIN

IT IS NOT STRANGE THAT THE VERY THING THAT YOU TRIED TO PREVENT HAS EMBRACED YOU AND WILL NOT LET YOU GO PAIN AND HURT

THERE ARE SO MANY TYPES OF PAIN SUCH AS

CHILD BIRTH

STOMPED TOE

BURN FROM COOKING OR

GUT WRENCHING CAN NOT GET OUT OF BED BALLED UP IN A FETAL POSITION PAIN THAT SEEMS TO GRIP YOU SO TIGHT THAT COMES FROM A PERSON DECEIVING YOU

DOES IT EVER STOP HURTING

IN TIME THE PAIN AND HURT THAT YOU FEEL DOES GO AWAY

IT TAKES TIME FOR WOUNDS TO HEAL

IT MAY TAKE DAYS WEEKS MONTHS OR YEARS

WHY DOES IT COME

WHEN YOU LOVE OR JUST LIVE THERE IS NO WAY THAT YOU CAN NOT EXPERIENCE SOME TYPE OF PAIN AND HURT

THAT IS A PART OF LIFE

THAT IS HARD BUT THERE IS NO WAY TO LIVE WITHOUT SOME PAIN AND HURT IN YOUR LIFE

DOES IT FEEL GOOD

IT DOES NOT FEEL GOOD WHEN YOU ARE IN PAIN AND HURT THAT YOU CAN FEEL DOWN TO THE MARROW OF YOUR BONES

YOU WEEP YOU MOAN YOU CAN NOT EAT CAN NOT SLEEP YET THE PAIN AND HURT STILL IS SO PROFOUND

HOW LONG WILL IT LAST

IT IS DIFFERENT WITH EACH EXPERIENCE AND WITH EACH PERSON

IT COULD BE SHORT TERM OR IT COULD BE LONG TERM

JUST KNOW THAT PAIN AND HURT DOES NOT LAST ALWAYS

WHAT OR HOW SHOULD I EXPRESS MY PAIN AND HURT

YOU CAN CRY SCREAM TALK JOG WALK READ A BOOK WRITE YOUR FEELINGS IN A JOURNAL

THERE ARE SO MANY WAYS TO SORT THIS OUT TO EASE THE PAIN AND HURT

DOES IT GET ANY BETTER

IT WILL IT SHALL GET BETTER AND EASIER TO DEAL WITH IN TIME

TIME HEALS ALL WOUNDS SOMEONE SAID AND THAT IS TRUE

ONE DAY YOU WILL WAKE UP AND THAT PAIN AND HURT THAT YOU FELT WILL BE LONG GONE JUST A VAGUE MEMORY

IT WILL NO LONGER HAUNT YOU

THE GOOD THING ABOUT PAIN AND HURT IT WILL ALLOW YOU TO KNOW AND UNDERSTAND YOUR TOLERANCE

THERE ARE GOING TO BE DIFFERENT LEVELS OF PAIN AND HURT BUT ENDURING EVERY STAGE ONLY HELPS YOU

IF IT DOES NOT KILL YOU IT WILL MAKE YOU STRONG SOMEONE SAID AND THAT IS TRUE

IT DOES NOT FEEL GOOD WHEN YOU GO THROUGH NEVERTHELESS GO

THROUGH AND COME OUT BETTER BRIGHTER WISER HAPPIER

BETTER ALL AROUND

WHEN YOU KNOW BETTER YOU WILL

LOVE LETTER TO ANTHONY AND TIFFANY

ANTHONY, TIFFANY

THE LOVE THAT A MOTHER HAS FOR HER CHILDREN IS ENDLESS.

RIGHT NOW I FEEL LIKE I HAVE DONE ALL THAT I CAN AND THEN SOME FOR YOU AND YOUR SISTER AND IT IS NOT ENOUGH.

THE MORE THAT I DO AND THE HARDER I WORK IT SEEMS TO ME THAT YOU ARE GOING IN ANOTHER DIRECTION

I NEED TO BE ABLE TO TRUST AND COUNT ON YOU IN CERTAIN SITUATIONS.

RIGHT NOW IT VERY DIFFICULT FOR ME HAVING TO WORK LIKE I AM

BUT IF I DO NOT DO IT THEN NO ONE WILL DO IT FOR US

I LOVE YOU AND TIFFANY WITH ALL OF MY HEART AND WITH ALL THAT IS WITHIN ME.

YES I GET UPSET BUT I CAN NEVER STOP LOVING AND CARING FOR YOU BOTH. I GAVE YOU LIFE AND NOW WE MUST WORK TOGETHER AND CONTINUE LIFE.

IT WILL ALL PAY OFF IN THE END JUST KNOW THAT ALL THAT I DO AND WILL EVER DO IS TO MAKE YOUR LIVES MUCH EASIER.

LOVE MOTHER

IS IT FAILURE

WHAT HAPPENS WHEN YOU DO NOT KNOW UP FROM DOWN

YOU CAN NOT SEEM TO GO ANYWHERE YOU ARE STUCK

YOU DO NOT EVEN HAVE ONE BUCK

IS IT FAILURE

WHEN YOU WANT TO LIE DOWN AND DIE

YOU DO NOT WANT TO PUT FORTH ANY EFFORT AND TRY

IS IT FAILURE

WHEN ALL YOU CAN SEE

IS WHAT YOU CAN NOT BE

ALL OF YOUR DREAMS RIGHT IN FRONT OF THEE

IS IT FAILURE

WHEN YOU TRY AND SPEAK GOOD

YET YOU ARE SO MISUNDERSTOOD

IS IT FAILURE

WHEN YOU HAVE MADE MISTAKE AFTER MISTAKE

ALL YOU WANT TO DO IS FIND THE NEAREST LAKE

IS IT FAILURE

WHEN YOU STOP CRYING

AND FEELING LIKE DYING

IS IT FAILURE

WHEN YOU NOW SEE

YOURSELF THE WAY YOU SHOULD BE

A SPECIAL GIFT FOR ALL TO SEE

BEING WITH YOU

BEING WITH YOU

MEANS THAT I AM NEVER BLUE

I FEEL SAFE WITH YOU

I JUST NEVER KNEW

THIS IS JUST ONE DAY

BUT I WOULD LIKE FOR THIS TO GO ON IF I HAD MY WAY

THINGS GET HARD FOR US

BUT IN YOU I PUT MY TRUST

BEING HERE FOR EACH OTHER IS THE WAY TO GO

IT IS PART OF HAVING, CARING, ENJOYING WHAT YOU KNOW

DESIRING FOR US TO BE TOGETHER JUST FEELS RIGHT

EVERYDAY WILL NOT BE SUNNY AND BRIGHT YET WE WILL NOT LOOSE SIGHT

YOU ARE ALL I WANT EACH DAY I WAKE

MY FEELINGS FOR YOU ARE REAL NEVER FAKE

I WANT TO SAY ROSES ARE RED AND VIOLETS ARE BLUE

LOVING YOU IS TRUE

EVERYDAY IT IS FRESH AND NEW

FOLLOW YOUR LEAD

I HAVE COME TO THE REALIZATION THAT NO MATTER WHAT I SAY OR DO NOT SAY I AM NEVER GOING TO MAKE YOU HAPPY

FOLLOW YOUR LEAD

I WILL NEVER BE YOUR WIFE AND THE CLOSEST THAT I WILL GET TO CARRYING YOUR NAME IS A PIECE OF MAIL I WAS HOLDING ON TO

FOLLOW YOUR LEAD

IN DOING A SELF CHECK I KNOW THAT I WAS OVER THE TOP INTENSE EXTREME WHEN IT CAME TO YOU HOWEVER, KNOWING THESE THINGS I CAN NOT APOLOGIZE BECAUSE ALL I EVER WANTED WAS YOU, I FELT LIKE YOU WERE THE MISSING PIECE IN MY LIFE

FOLLOW YOUR LEAD

I FOUND MYSELF PUTTING TOO MUCH ENERGY INTO WHY DIDN'T HE CALL? WHY DIDN'T HE TEXT? WHY DOESN'T HE SEE HOW EASY IT IS FOR US TO BE TOGETHER?

FOLLOW YOUR LEAD

IT WOULD REALLY TROUBLE ME WITH ALL THE WHY OR WHY NOTS THAT WOULD PLACE ME IN A DOWNWARD SPIRAL I COULD NOT SEEM TO FUNCTION WITHOUT THE ANTICIPATION THE HOPE THE EXPECTATION OF KNOWING WE WILL SEE EACH OTHER WE WILL TALK OR TEXT

FOLLOW YOUR LEAD

I HAD IT SO BAD I WOULD GO TO BED WITH YOU ON MY MIND AND WAKE UP THE SAME AND EVEN DREAM OF YOU THROUGHOUT THE NIGHT

FOLLOW YOUR LEAD

THE REALITY IS I KNOW THAT I PUT AN EXTREME AMOUNT INTO EVERYTHING ABOUT US FROM KEEPING RECEIPTS, KEEPING BAGS THAT GIFTS CAME OUT OF, KEEPING FLOWERS THAT NO LONGER HAVE LIFE, TO TEXTS AND I CAN GO ON AND ON AND ON

FOLLOW YOUR LEAD

YOU TRIED TO TELL ME THAT YOU WERE NOT THE MAN FOR ME BUT ALL I COULD SEE WAS HOW YOU MADE ME FEEL AND HOW COULD THAT BE SO WRONG TO WANT TO BE WITH YOU

FOLLOW YOUR LEAD

I WAS SO CONSUMED WITH YOU AND WANTING MORE AND MORE I FELT LIKE EVENTUALLY YOU WOULD FEEL THE SAME BUT NOT SO KNOWING THAT YOU WILL NEVER ACKNOWLEGE THIS AS HOME AND US BUILDING A LIFE TOGETHER SHOULD HAVE BEEN A CLUE WHEN YOU SAID YOU COULD NOT HELP WITH THE BILLS I STILL MADE A FOOL OF MYSELF BY TRYING WHATEVER I COULD TO CHANGE YOUR MIND FOOLISH IS HOW I HAVE BEEN ACTING

FOLLOW YOUR LEAD

YOU HAVE A LIFE AND FRIENDS I WAS THE ONE SO FOCUSED ON TRYING TO PLEASE YOU AND MAKE SOMETHING HAPPEN THAT OBVIOUSLY YOU DO NOT FEEL THE SAME ABOUT

FOLLOW YOUR LEAD

I CAN NOT APOLOGIZE FOR MY FEELING BECAUSE WANTING TO GET TO KNOW YOU WANTING TO SEE YOU WANTING TO LOVE WITHOUT FEAR WANTING TO SHARE WANTING WANTING WANTING MORE WAS NEVER A GOOD THING

FOLLOW YOUR LEAD

SO RIGHT NOW I AM FOLLOWING YOUR LEAD IF YOU CALL TEXT OR COME BY OK AND IF YOU DON'T CALL TEXT OR COME BY OK I HAVE

FOCUSED ON THE WRONG THINGS FOR SO LONG UNTIL IT BECAME HABIT WORRYING ABOUT THINGS I CAN NOT CHANGE OR CONTROL

FOLLOW YOUR LEAD

YOU ARE GOING TO DO WHAT YOU WANT WHEN YOU WANT WITH WHOM YOU WANT AND THAT HAS ALWAYS BEEN THE WAY IT IS AND I AM NO LONGER GOING TO FUSS ARGUE OR BICKER WITH YOU NO MATTER WHAT I DO OR SAY IT WILL NEVER BE ENOUGH AND ONCE YOU GET YOUR MIND FIXED ON SOMETHING RIGHT OR WRONG THAT IS THE WAY IT IS

FOLLOW YOUR LEAD

SOMEHOW I HAVE DID OR SAID SOMETHING OR I DID NOT DO OR SAY SOMETHING THAT LANDED ME HERE WITH YOU

YOU SAID EVERYTHING WAS OK BUT I DID NOT GET THE GOOD NIGHT TEXT BUT I HAVE DONE ALL THAT I KNOW TO DO AND SAY TO LET YOU KNOW HOW I FEEL THIS SEEMS LIKE SOME MADE UP MESS IN ORDER FOR YOU TO DO WHAT YOU REALLY WANTED TO DO AND THAT CAN NOT BE CHANGED SO I MUST FOLLOW YOUR LEAD

FOLLOW YOUR LEAD

I AM STILL TRYING TO UNDERSTAND HOW THINGS GO FROM GREAT IN MY MIND TO THIS BUT HERE AGAIN I CAN NOT CONCERN MYSELF WITH THINGS I CAN NOT CHANGE OR CONTROL I TOOK IT UPON MYSELF TO ASSUME AND I AM AND HAVE MADE AN A.. OUT OF MYSELF SO MANY TIMES UNTIL

FOLLOW YOUR LEAD

I HAVE TRIED BEING IN A RELATIONSHIP TWICE AND BOTH TIMES IT FAILED SO I CAN ONLY LOOK AT MYSELF AS THE BLAME BUT WHEN MY HEART IS HURTING AFTER I HAVE TRIED SO HARD WHERE DO HOW DO WHEN DOES THE PAIN STOP SO I CAN MOVE FORWARD

FOLLOW YOUR LEAD

HOW CAN LOVING SOMEONE AND WANTING TO BE WITH THEM
WANTING TO EXPERIENCE NEW AND DIFFERENT THINGS EXCITING
THINGS BE SO WRONG? HOW CAN BEING OPEN AND HONEST BE SO
WRONG? HOW CAN THINKING OF YOU AND PUTTING YOUR NEEDS
BEFORE MINE BE SO WRONG? HOW CAN LYING AWAKE AT NIGHT
THINKING OF HOW WONDERFUL A PERSON BE SO WRONG? HOW CAN
BEING HEAD OVER HEELS FOR YOU BE SO WRONG?   WHAT HAVE I
DONE THAT IS SO WRONG FOR ME TO HURT THIS WAY WHATEVER IT IS
GOD KNOWS I WILL NEVER DO IT AGAIN STOP THE PAIN

FOLLOW YOUR LEAD

I AM GOING TO TRY THINGS THIS WAY NOT EXPECTING ANYTHING NOT
HOPING FOR ANYTHING AND NOT ANTICIPATING ANYTHING AND
WHEN I CAN NO LONGER DO THIS I WILL WALK AWAY KNOWING THAT
WHEN YOU GIVE YOUR BEST AND YOUR ALL UNTIL IT HURTS WHAT
EVER HAPPENS IS FOR THE BEST

GREAT TIMES

BECAUSE OF YOUR BIRTH OUR WORLDS CAME TOGETHER

BECAUSE OF YOU I FEEL ALIVE WHEN I THINK OF YOU AND WHEN WE ARE TOGETHER AND I LONG FOR YOU WHEN WE ARE APART WONDERING WHAT YOU ARE DOING AND IF YOU FEEL THE SAME

BECAUSE OF YOU WHEN WE ARE NOT SPEAKING TO EACH OTHER TEARS STREAM AND I FEEL LIKE THE PART OF ME THAT I THRIVE ON AND FROM IS MISSING AND DO NOT LIKE THE FEELING OF ME WITHOUT YOU, THE US FACTOR

BECAUSE OF YOU I AM ABLE TO EXPRESS MYSELF IN WAYS I NEVER FELT POSSIBLE

BECAUSE OF YOU I CAN NOT SAY NO TO YOU YET YOU DO NOT SEEM TO UNDERSTAND THE MEANING OF THAT WORD

BECAUSE OF YOU WHEN YOU ARE CONTAGIOUS AND WANT TO PASS ON YOUR GERMS I ENJOY GETTINTG YOUR GERMS

BECAUSE OF YOU PUTTING AWAY OR LOADING THE WARES CAN LEAD TO GREAT TIMES

BECAUSE OF YOU I WOULD RATHER BE WORKING IN THE GARDEN AND GETTING DIRTY THAN ANY PLACE ELSE ON THIS EARTH

BECAUSE OF YOU SPENDING TIME LONG OR SHORT MEANS SO VERY MUCH

BECAUSE OF YOU I WILL NEVER LOVE ANYONE THE WAY THAT I LOVE YOU

BECAUSE OF YOU ALL THINGS BIG AND SMALL WILL BE CHERISHED

BECAUSE OF YOU MY LIFE WILL NEVER BE THE SAME

BECAUSE OF YOU I HAVE IMAGINED SPENDING THE REST OF OUR LIVES

TOGETHER WHAT IT WOULD BE LIKE TO GO TO BED AND WAKE UP
WITH YOU UNTIL LIFE HAS LEFT US BOTH

BECAUSE OF YOUR BIRTH AND OUR WORLDS CAME TOGTHER GOOD
AND BAD YOU MEAN SO MUCH TO ME

MY WISH FOR YOU ON YOUR BIRTHDAY AND ALWAYS THAT YOU ARE
GETTING ALL THAT YOU WANT AND DESIRE IN YOUR LIFE

HAPPY 13TH BIRTHDAY TO MY SON

HAPPY 13TH BIRTHDAY TO MY SON

FOR YOU THE RACE HAS JUST BEGUN

YOU ARE SPECIAL AND VERY DEAR

I AM RAISING YOU TO HAVE NO FEAR

FOR JESUS CHRIST IS ALWAYS NEAR

HAVE FUN ON THIS YOUR DAY

KEEP THE MEMORIES AND DO NOT LET THEM SLIP AWAY

I LOVE YOU AND THAT IS ALWAYS

HAPPY BIRTHDAY IT GOES AWAY IT NEVER STAYS

I SEE YOU AS A GREAT MAN TO BE

I GAVE BIRTH TO YOU ON THIS DAY AND SEEMS LIKE ONLY YESTERDAY

YOU ARE DESTINED FOR WONDERFUL THINGS KEEP LIVING AND YOU WILL SEE

HAPPY 13TH BIRTHDAY MY SON

HOW COULD

HOW COULD SOMETHING SO RIGHT GO WRONG

WHEN YOU WAKE UP THANK GOD FOR THE DAY AND THE PEOPLE IN IT

YOUR THOUGHTS TURN TO HIM

HOW COULD SOMETHING SO RIGHT GO WRONG

YOU MAKE YOUR PRESENCE KNOWN AND HE HAS CAPTURED YOUR UNDIVIDED ATTENTION

HOW COULD SOMETHING SO RIGHT GO WRONG

THE PLAN FOR THE DAY IS TO SEE EACH OTHER SPEND QUALITY TIME TOGETHER

HOW COULD SOMETHING SO RIGHT GO WRONG

EVERYTHING IS GOING LIKE A NICE SPRING BREEZE

ALL OF A SUDDEN THE BOTTOM FALLS OUT

HOW COULD SOMETHING SO RIGHT GO WRONG

YOU NORMALLY WOULD NOT CARE HOW THIS TURNS OUT

BUT YOU NOW WANT THINGS TO WORK OUT FOR THE GOOD

HOW COULD SOMETHING SO RIGHT GO WRONG

YOU DESPERATELY TRY TO MAKE IT WORK YET DEEP IN YOUR HEART YOU DO NOT WANT TO SEEM ANY MORE FOOLISH

HOW COULD SOMETHING SO RIGHT GO WRONG

WHAT IS IT

HOW CAN THIS BE REPAIRED

WHAT HAPPENED

PLEASE HELP ME TO UNDERSTAND WHAT WENT WRONG

TALK TO ME

COMMUNICATE THE ISSUE WITH ME SO WE CAN FIX IT YET NOTHING

HOW COULD SOMETHING SO RIGHT GO WRONG

YOU ARE TRYING ALL THAT YOU KNOW TO GET THIS BACK ON TRACK
BECAUSE YOU WANT TO LOOK INTO THOSE BROWN EYES AGAIN

HOW COULD SOMETHING SO RIGHT GO WRONG

AT THIS POINT YOU ARE TRYING TO REPLAY THE EVENTS OVER IN YOUR
MIND TO SEE WHERE THINGS WENT WRONG

HOW COULD SOMETHING SO RIGHT GO WRONG

YOU ASSUME IT IS THIS OR THAT AND TRY TO PATCH IT UP FROM THERE
AND TO NO AVAIL

HOW COULD SOMETHING SO RIGHT GO WRONG

NOW YOU ARE BASICALLY GRASPING AT STRAWS

YOU WANT THIS MORE THAN ANYTHING AND SOMEHOW YOU CAN
NOT SEEM TO GET THIS TO WORK

HOW COULD SOMETHING SO RIGHT GO WRONG

YOU DO EVERYTHING YOU CAN WITHOUT SEEMING AS IF A PERSON
OUT OF CONTROL BUT AT THIS POINT YOU FEEL YOU ARE OUT THERE
AND THERE IS NO TURNING BACK

HOW COULD SOMETHING SO RIGHT GO WRONG

NOW THAT YOU HAVE REGAINED YOUR COMPOSURE

YOU RE-EXAM OR RE-VISIT THE SITUATION AND YOU CONCLUDE THAT

MAYBE THIS WAS NOT ALL THAT TO BEGIN WITH

HOW COULD SOMETHING SO RIGHT GO WRONG

ALL OF THE GOOD TIMES DID YOU IMAGINE THAT

DO YOU REALLY CARE FOR ONE ANOTHER

IS THIS REALISTIC

WHY ARE YOU SPENDING TIME WITH EACH OTHER

WHY ARE WE UNABLE TO WORK THROUGH THIS

WAS THIS MEANT TO BE

WHEN YOUR HANDS TOUCHED WAS IT REALLY MAGICAL

IS THERE A FUTURE HERE

HOW COULD SOMETHING SO RIGHT GO WRONG

YOU SHOULD JUST BE SILENT AND ALLOW THINGS TO TAKE ITS COURSE

HOW COULD SOMETHING SO RIGHT GO WRONG

YOU CAN HONESTLY SAY THAT NO MATTER WHAT COMES OR GOES
YOU GAVE THIS YOUR ALL

NO REGRETS

HOW COULD SOMETHING SO RIGHT GO WRONG

REMEMBER ALL THE GOOD TIMES

KEEP POSITIVE THOUGHTS

DO THINGS THAT MAKE YOU HAPPY

ALL GOOD THINGS HAVE TO COME TO AN END YET IN YOUR HEART
THEY NEVER WILL

YOU DO NOT WANT TO LET GO BUT YOU KNOW IT IS FOR THE BEST

HOW COULD SOMETHING SO RIGHT GO WRONG

YOU WANT TO GO BACK TO THE GREAT TIMES THAT YOU SHARED

LAUGH LIVE AND LOVE WITH THAT PERSON

HOW COULD SOMETHING SO RIGHT GO WRONG

YOU TRY TO CONVINCE YOUR SELF THAT HE WAS NOT THE ONE

THIS WAS NOT MEANT TO BE

HE WAS NOT YOUR DESTINY HE WAS JUST A STOP A LONG THE WAY

ANY OTHER THING THAT WILL BRING YOU SOME COMFORT

YET HOWEVER MOREOVER

YOU JUST WANT TO TALK THIS OUT AND GET BACK ON TRACK

HOW COULD SOMETHING SO RIGHT GO WRONG

YOU WONDER WHAT HE IS DOING WHILE YOU TWO ARE APART

DOES HE THINK OF YOU

DOES HE MISS YOU

DOES HE FEEL LIKE THE BETTER PART OF HIM IS MISSING

DOES HE WANT THIS TO WORK

HAS HE MOVED ON

HAS HE REPLACED YOU

DID HE DO THIS TO GET OUT OF WHAT YOU TWO HAD TOGETHER

DOES HE WANT TO CALL TEXT OR E-MAIL

IS HE CONTENT WITH THINGS THE WAY THEY HAVE TURNED OUT

HOW COULD SOMETHING SO RIGHT GO WRONG

YOU ARE TORN

DO YOU BREAK DOWN CALL TEXT OR E-MAIL

DO YOU STAY STRONG AND IF HE WANTS TO CALL TEXT OR E-MAIL HE WILL AND LEAVE IT AT THAT

HOW COULD SOMETHING SO RIGHT GO WRONG

YOU HAVE COME TO THE RESOLVE THAT LOVE IS NOT FOR YOU

YOU HAVE TRIED IT AND YES IT DOES NOT FEEL GOOD AFTER SHARING SO MANY GOOD TIMES AND GOING THROUGH SOME ROUGH TIMES WITH SOMEONE AND DOES IT END HERE

BE STRONG CRY IF NEEDED BUT KEEP YOUR HEAD UP

HOW COULD SOMETHING SO RIGHT GO WRONG

IT IS OK TO HURT BUT DO NOT STAY THERE

KEEP MOVING

DO THINGS TO KEEP YOURSELF FEELING GOOD AND LOOKING GOOD

STOP EATING CHOCOLATE AND ICE CREAM

JOG WALK EXERCISE

DO NOT LET YOURSELF GO INSTEAD PICK YOURSELF UP AND STAY THERE

THINK POSITIVE READ AND PRAY

LOVE GOD ALWAYS HE WILL NEVER LEAVE YOU NOR FORSAKE YOU

HOW DID I GET HERE

THEY MEET WITH A PASSIONATE KISS AS SHE IS LOOKING INTO HIS EYES
AND THEIR BODIES PRESSED TOGETHER SHE THINKS TO HERSELF

HOW DID I GET HERE

SHE RECALLS THEIR FIRST MEETINGS AND AT SOME POINT HE SAID
SOMETHING TO CAPTURE HER ATTENTION YET

HOW DID I GET HERE

SHE IS AWARE OF WHAT SHE IS GETTING INTO BUT NONETHELESS SHE
VENTURES OUT AND TAKES THE PLUNG

HOW DID I GET HERE

WHEN THINGS ARE GOOD BETWEEN THEM THEY ARE REALLY GOOD
AND WHEN THEY ARE NOT IT SADDENS HER TO NO END

HOW DID I GET HERE

THEY ARE TRULY GOOD FOR ONE ANOTHER TO THE POINT THEY MESH
SO WELL THEY ARE REALLY GOOD TOGETHER FOR EACH OTHER AND
GOOD TO EACH OTHER

HOW DID I GET HERE

SHE NEVER THOUGH IN HER WILDEST DREAMS THAT THIS COULD BE
THE ONE THAT TAKES HER FROM HER SHELL IT'S LIKE THE CATERPILLAR
TO THE BUTTERFLY

HOW DID I GET HERE

SHE ANTICIPATES HEARING FROM HIM NOT KNOWING WHEN AND
KNOWING THAT THERE WOULD BE TIMES SUCH AS THESE YET SHE CAN
NOT SEEM TO LET HIM GO AND WHEN SHE TRIES SHE ALWAYS COMES
BACK KNOWING THAT THIS WILL CONTINUE TO HAPPEN

HOW DID I GET HERE

SHE HAS OPENED UP WITH HIM IN WAYS SHE NEVER COULD HAVE
IMAGINED AND HAS ENJOYED EVERY MINUTE OF IT

HOW DID I GET HERE

IN HER MIND HE IS THE ONE THAT SHE WANTS IN HER LIFE NOW AND
ALWAYS HOWEVER SHE KNOWS THAT NO MATTER HOW THEY FEEL
ABOUT EACH OTHER HE HAS OPTIONS AND HER PROBLEM IS SHE LOVES
HIM AND ONLY WANTS TO BE WITH HIM AND IN HER MIND THAT IS
ENOUGH BUT THE REALITY IS SHE WILL ALWAYS WANT WHAT SHE CAN
NOT HAVE

HOW DID I GET HERE

THE WAY HE MAKES HER FEEL IS LIKE FEELINGS SHE NEVER FELT BEFORE
AND NEVER WANTS THAT TO END

HOW DID I GET HERE

WHEN THEY ARE TOGETHER THERE IS NO PLACE THEY WOULD RATHER
BE THAN EMBRACING ONE ANOTHER

HOW DID I GET HERE

SHE SAID THAT SHE KNEW WHAT SHE WAS GETTING HERSELF INTO BUT
SHE REALLY HAD NO IDEA THAT IT COULD POSSIBLY BE THIS WAY

HOW DID I GET HERE

SHE TRIED TO LEAVE HIM MANY TIMES BECAUSE DEEP DOWN INSIDE
SHE REALIZES THAT THE FUTURE SHE WANTS CAN NOT BE WITH HIM

HOW DID I GET HERE

SHE DENIED TO HIM AND ALL THE WHILE SHE HAD TO BE HONEST WITH
HERSELF AND SHE WANTS WHAT CAN NEVER BE HERS

HOW DID I GET HERE

AS FAR AS SHE CAN REMEMBER SHE HAS NEVER WANTED WHAT SOMEONE HAD

SHE ONLY WANTED WHAT SHE WANTED

HOW DID I GET HERE

THE MAN THAT SHE DESIRES AND LOVES SO DEEPLY CAN NEVER BE WITH HER BECAUSE HE BELONGS TO SOMEONE ELSE

HOW DID I GET HERE

SHE LONGS TO BE WITH HIM AND THEY ENJOY THE TIME THAT IS SHARED HOWEVER, SHE KNOWS THAT SHE WILL NEVER BE ALL THAT HE WANTS AND DESIRES

HOW DID I GET HERE

REALLY AND TRULY SHE COULD NOT HAVE KNOWN THAT BEING WITH HIM WOULD FLOURISH INTO WHAT THEY HAVE BETWEEN THEM

HOW DID I GET HERE

SHE KNOWS THAT THE MORE TIME THAT THEY SHARE HOW DIFFICULT THINGS COULD GET AND SOMEHOW SHE CAN NOT SEEM TO LET HIM GO

HOW DID I GET HERE

DOES SHE GO OR DOES SHE STAY WITH A MAN THAT COULD NEVER BE HERS WITHOUT HIM MAKES HER LIFE SO MISERABLE BUT WITH HIM SHE FEELS A LIVE FULL OF ALL THAT IS GOOD

HOW DID I GET HERE

SHE IS IN SO DEEP WITH HIM SHE DREAMS OF HIM WHEN THEY ARE NOT TOGETHER AND WANTS TO BE WHEREVER HE IS

HOW DID I GET HERE

SHE TRIED LIVING WITHOUT THE MAN THAT MAKES HER FEEL ALIVE MORE TIMES THAN SHE CARES TO COUNT BUT THEY ALWAYS SEEM TO WORK THEIR WAY BACK TO EACH OTHER

SHE THINKS ABOUT COULD SHE DO THE SAME TO HER THAT SHE IS DOING TO SOMEONE ELSE BUT IN THE END SHE CARES BUT WHAT IS MOST GROUNDING FOR HER IS THAT SHE LOVES THIS MAN AND WANTS TO BE WITH HIM NO MATTER WHAT

HOW DID I GET HERE

SHE DOES WONDER HOW DOES SOMETHING SO WRONG FEEL SO RIGHT TO HER SHE WONDERS THIS VERY THING OFTEN

HOW DID I GET HERE

HOW COULD THE MAN OF HER DREAMS BE SOMEONE ELSES YET SHE FEELS AS IF HE IS HERS AT TIMES AND THEN REALITY SETS IN AND SHE KNOWS THAT FOR THAT TIME SHE WANTED IT TO BE SO

HOW DID I GET HERE

IF THE TRUTH MUST BE TOLD HERE IS WHERE SHE WANTS TO BE AS CRAZY AS THAT MAY SEEM THIS PLACE IS A PLACE SHE HAS NEVER KNOWN AND WANTS TO ENJOY IT WHILE SHE CAN

HOW DID I GET HERE

SHE KNOWS THAT WHEN THEY ARE NOT TOGETHER HE COULD BE WITH ANOTHER AND THIS IS EXACTLY WHY SHE KNOWS THAT THIS COULD NEVER BE THE MAN THAT SHE COULD SPEND THE REST OF LIFE WITH

HOW DID I GET HERE

SHE TRIES TO NOT LET IT BOTHER HER NEVERTHELESS, SHE GOES THROUGHOUT EACH DAY WITH THIS QUESTION IS HE OR ISN'T HE AND SHE CAN NOT LIVE LIKE THIS

HOW DID I GET HERE

SHE REMEMBERS READING ABOUT SOME WISE WOMEN AND SOME
FOOLISH WOMEN AND WHEN SHE JUST SAT DOWN AND WAS HONEST
WITH HERSELF TRULY HONEST SHE KNOWS THAT SHE IS FOOLISH

HOW DID I GET HERE

HOW SHE FEELS THIS WAY ABOUT A MAN THAT SHE KNOWS COULD
NEVER BE HERS TOTALLY SHE CAN NOT SAY

THAT IS WHY SHE WANTS TO KNOW

HOW DID I GET HERE

I AM BLUE WITHOUT YOU

I NEED A HUG AND KISS

WITHOUT IT THERE IS NO BLISS

I AM BLUE WITHOUT YOU

I NEED TO LOOK INTO YOUR EYES

I WANT TO FEEL THAT WE HAVE TIES AND NOT JUST LIES

I AM BLUE WITHOUT YOU

I NEED TO HOLD YOUR HAND

IN ORDER TO TRY TO COMPREHNED WHERE WE STAND

I AM BLUE WITHOUT YOU

I WANT YOU TO TASTE ME

TAKE ME PLACES THAT I NEVER THOUGHT A REALITY

I AM BLUE WITHOUT YOU

I DESIRE TO PLEASE YOU BEYOND MEASURE

WITH YOU I WILL FIND MY TREASURE

TOGETHER WE HAVE SO MUCH PLEASURE

I AM BLUE WITHOUT YOU

LET US LOVE EACH OTHER UNTIL THE END OF TIME

BASKING INTO A REALM OF ENDLESS HOPES DREAMS AND FANTASIES FAR BEYOND OUR DEEPEST THOUGHTS WITHOUT ANY REASON OR RHYME

I AM BLUE WITHOUT YOU

I CAN ONLY WONDER IF YOU FEEL THE SAME WAY TOO

ARE YOU BLUE WITHOUT ME

CAN THAT BE TRUE

LIFE GOES ON

ON THIS JOURNEY THERE WILL BE GOOD AND BAD HAPPY AND SAD

LIFE GOES ON

TO LAUGH AND TO CRY

NOT REALIZING WITH LOVE YOU MUST TRY

LIFE GOES ON

IT IS ALWAYS EASY TO FOLLOW YOUR HEART

IT IS NOT EASY TO HAVE TO RESTART

LIFE GOES ON

THERE IS A TIME AND SEASON FOR EVERYTHING

AND FOR A TIME I COULD HEAR MY HEART SING AND SING

LIFE GOES ON

ENJOYING THE TIME THAT WAS SHARED

NOTHING ELSE COMAPARED

LIFE GOES ON

WHEN ONE GOES THOUGH LIFE AS AN EMPTY SHELL

AND WHEN THIS JOY COMES IT LIKE A BURST WELL

LIFE GOES ON

TO GIVE OF YOURSELF LIKE NEVER BEFORE

MAKES YOU FEEL AS IF TIME SHARED ON A SEA SHORE

LIFE GOES ON

YOU REPLAY IN YOUR MIND THE TIMES THAT WERE SHARED

YET SOMEHOW YOUR VISION WAS IMPAIRED

LIFE GOES ON

IF ONLY THERE WERE TWO OF THIS PERSON

THAT WAY THERE IS NO TIME LIMIT ON THE FUN

LIFE GOES ON

THE HEART CAN NO LONGER BE TRUSTED

RIGHT NOT YOU ARE BUSTED

LIFE GOES ON

IF ONLY YOU LISTENED WITH YOUR EARS AND NOT YOUR HEART

AT THIS POINT YOU WOULD FEEL SMART

LIFE GOES ON

THAT TIME WILL ALWAYS BE CHERISHED

NOW IT'S YOUR HEART THAT NEEDS TO BE

NOURISHED

WILL LIFE GO ON BECAUSE RIGHT NOW THE WEIGHT FEELS LIKE A TON

LONG DISTANCE LOVE

LOVE CAN HAPPEN DAY OR NIGHT

IT CAN HAPPEN AND IT FEELS JUST RIGHT

NEVER COULD IT BE IMAGINED THAT LOVING YOU COULD BE SO EASY

YOU CAN NOT STOP SPINNING YOU FEEL QUEEZY

IS THERE A GOOD TIME A PREPARED TIME OR A PERFECT TIME TO FALL IN LOVE

WHO KNOWS BUT WHEN YOU ARE THERE YOU FEEL FREE LIKE A DOVE

WANTING TO BE WITH A PERSON WHO IS MILES A WAY

YOU WANT THEM CLOSE NEVER TO LEAVE JUST STAY

DO YOU KEEP UP THE FIGHT

OR DO YOU SAY THIS IS NOT WORKING AND TAKE FLIGHT

DEEP DOWN YOU KNOW THAT WOULD NOT BE RIGHT

YOU JUST WANT THEM IN YOUR SIGHT

DO YOU SAY I HAVE LOVED AGAIN AND NOW IT TIME TO SAY GOOD BYE

BREAKING THE LONG DISTANCE TIE

IF LOVING SOMEONE WAS EASY EVERYONE WOULD HAVE SOMEONE

ENJOYING EACH OTHER HAVING FUN UNDER THE SUN

NOT FEELING LIKE A HEAVY WEIGHT A TON

THERE ARE THINGS IN LIFE WORTH WAITING FOR

IN ORDER TO MAKE THE REALTIONSHIP SOAR

LOVING SOMEONE OTHER THAN ONE'S SELF

LOVE IS PATIENT BEING ABLE TO SEE THE GOOD

AND WONDERING HOW THEY COULD

LOVE IS KIND ALLOWING YOURSELF TO REACH OUT

SOMETIMES NOT KNOWING WHAT THEY ARE ABOUT

LOVE IS STRONG

BEING THERE WHEN EVERYTHING GOES WRONG

LOVE IS BLIND NOT LOOKING AT WHAT IS IN FRONT OF YOU

BUT SEEING THEM AS BEAUTIFUL AND NEW

LOVE IS MANY THINGS

AND ONE CAN BE CONTENT WITH ALL THE JOY THAT BRINGS

MY DAUGHTER TIFFANY MY LOVE

TIFFANY YOU ARE MY DAUGHTER AND MY LOVE

FROM THE MOMENT THAT I KNEW I HAD CONCEIVED YOU (EVEN BEFORE) I LOVED YOU SO MUCH

ONCE YOU WERE BORN HEALTHY AND HAPPY I KNEW THAT WE WOULD BE CLOSE AND SHARE MANY THINGS AS FEMALES

MY DAUGHTER TIFFANY MY LOVE

PLEASE KNOW THAT NO MATTER WHAT PATH YOU TAKE IN THIS LIFE ALL I WANT FOR YOU IS THE BEST

I WILL MAKE NO APOLOGIES FOR WANTING AND DESIRING THE BEST FOR YOU

TIME WILL PASS AND YOU WILL GROW INTO THE YOUNG LADY OF GOD THAT I KNOW YOU WERE BORN TO BE

MY DAUGHTER TIFFANY MY LOVE

YOU ARE HUMAN AND WILL MAKE MISTAKES AND THAT IS OKAY, HOWEVER, LEARNING FROM YOUR MISTAKES AND MUCH PRAYER WILL TAKE YOU FAR IN LIFE

MY DAUGHTER TIFFANY MY LOVE

I WILL NEVER HAVE ANOTHER DAUGHTER YOU ARE ALL I NEED

YOU ARE BEAUTIFUL, SMART, CREATIVE, AND DETERMINED. AS WELL AS HEAD STRONG AND STRONG WILLED

I LOVE YOU MORE THAN YOU WILL EVER KNOW

MY DAUGHTER TIFFANY MY LOVE

OUR TIME TOGETHER

ALL I WANTED WAS FOR US TO LOVE EACH OTHER AND DO RIGHT BY EACH OTHER AND CONTINUE TO BUILD UPON WHAT WE HAVE YET FOR SOME REASON THAT WILL NEVER HAPPEN. HOW CAN IT BE THAT WHEN I LOOK AT YOU OR THINK OF YOU MY HEART LEAPS WITH JOY AND WHEN YOU SEE OR THINK OF ME IT IS JUST TIME OR IT HAS NO MEANING? I CAN TELL YOU WHY MY FEELINGS FOR YOU RUN DEEPER THAN YOU CAN EVER IMAGINE AND I AM NOW SEEING THINGS THE WAY THAT YOU ARE WITH CLEAR AND OPEN EYES. I WILL NEVER MAKE THIS MISTAKE AGAIN AND THAT YOU CAN COUNT ON.

YOU SAY THAT YOU CAN NOT MAKE A DECISION YET EVERY TIME WE ARE TOGETHER AND WITHOUT HESITATION YOU MAKE DECISIONS BY DOING THIS AND THAT. YOU HAVE MADE A DECISION.

ALTHOUGH YOU CLAIM YOU CAN NOT YOU DO IT VERY WELL

I HAVE COME TO REALIZE THAT THERE IS NO WAY THAT YOU COULD HAVE EVER LOVED ME, RESPECTED ME OR APPRECIATED ME BECAUSE OF YOUR ACTIONS. SOMEHOW I FELT AS IF YOU CARED TO SOME DEGREE BUT THAT IS OBVIOUSLY NOT THE CASE AT ALL. I ADMIT I ALLOWED YOU TO TREAT ME AS IF I WAS JUST SOMETHING TO DO BUT I CAN NO LONGER DO THAT.

OUR TIME ONLY EXSIST IN MY MIND BECAUSE AS FAR AS YOU ARE CONCERNED IT IS JUST TIME AND THAT IS MY FAULT FOR CHERISHING AND WANTING THE TIME THAT WE SHARE TO BE VIEWED AS SPECIAL. THAT IS WHAT I GET FOR ASSUMING YES I MADE AN A... OF MYSELF. I WILL ALWAYS REMEMBER THIS WEEKEND AS THE WEEKEND I MADE MYSELF LOOK LIKE THE BIGGEST FOOL EVER. YOU HAVE NO CARES OR WORRIES BECAUSE YOU ARE GETTING ALL THAT YOU WANT.

I WAS PREPARED TO SPEND THE REST OF MY LIFE DEALING WITH THIS FOOLISHNESS JUST SO I COULD BE A PART OF YOUR WORLD BUT I AM NO LONGER WILLING TO BE VIEWED AS AN IGNORANT WOMAN.

THE VESTED TIME THAT YOU ARE COMMITTEED TO, THE DEDICATION
TO THE PHONE AND IT IS YOUR MONEY AND THE FEELINGS THAT ARE
DEEP ROOTED IS APPEARANTLY WHAT YOU WANT BECAUSE WITHOUT
FAIL IT IS ALWAYS PRESENT AND ACCOUNTED FOR BY YOU.

YOU HAD AN URGENCY TO GO AND THAT WAS A DECISION THAT I WILL
AGREE WITH YOU ON   JUST GO!

REFLECTING

WHEN REFLECTING BACK ON THIS PAST TWELVE MONTHS IT CAN BE SAID THAT WE HAVE ENDURED QUITE AN TREMENDOUS AMOUNT OF UPS AND DOWNS

THIS ROAD OR THIS JOURNEY TOGETHER HAS BEEN BOTH BITTER AND SWEET HARD AND SOFT

REALIZING WITH YOU AND ABOUT YOU IS THAT YOU HAVE BEEN WORTH ALL OF IT

THE FACT IS IF GOING THROUGH HARD TIMES AND EMBRACING THE GOOD ONES FEELS LIKE THIS THERE WILL BE MANY YEARS THAT ARE TO BE CELEBRATED

LOOKING BACK ON THIS JOURNEY AND HOW IT ALMOST NEVER MANIFESTED BECAUSE OF CIRCUMSTANCES AND SITUATIONS GOING ON AROUND US

THERE WILL ALWAYS BE A DEEP AND PASSIONATE CARE FOR YOU

YOU CHALLENGED US TO FACE OUR INNER FEARS AND GET BEYOND THEM

PLEASE KNOW THAT YOU BRING OUT THINGS INSIDE THAT WERE HIDDEN SO DEEPLY THAT IT WAS NOT KNOWN THAT THINGS COULD EVER BE EXPRESSED OPENLY AND FREELY

YOU ARE WANTED MORE AND MORE

YOU MAY NEVER KNOW THAT TRULY YOU HAVE SUCH VALUE THAT CAN NOT BE EMPHASIZED ENOUGH

AT TIMES IT WAS DIFFICULT TO SHARE AND TO OPEN UP YET THERE YOU WERE WITH THE PATIENCE THAT WAS NEEDED AND DESIRED

DAILY WORDS OF THANKS AND APPRECIATION FOR WHAT HAS BEEN

THAT DRAWS OR BINDS US CLOSER AND CLOSER

NOT KNOWING WHERE THIS IS HEADED CAN BE A LITTLE UNSETTTLING
AT TIME BUT THE MEMORIES THAT WE HAVE HOLD SUCH SIGNIFICANCE

LEARNING AND GROWING TOGETHER IS ALL APART OF BEING IN A
REALTIONSHIP AND IT FEELS REMARKABLE TO HAVE THIS WITH YOU

ALL IN ALL THIS HAS BEEN A VOYAGE OF A LIFETIME AND WOULD NOT
HAVE MEANT AS MUCH IF IT HAD NOT BEEN WITH YOU NOT WANTING
THIS TO EVER END

EVERY NOW AND THEN THIS FEELS LIKE A DREAM AND PLEASE ALLOW
THE DREAM TO CONTINUE WITHOUT ANY INTERRUPTION

THE TIMES WE SHARED THE LAUGHTER THE COMING TOGETHER THE
PLANS THAT WERE MADE ALL OF THESE THINGS ARE VERY DEAR

MORE OVER THIS YEAR HAS ALLOWED US TO ESTABLISH A FIRM
FOUNDATION FOR WHAT MAY BE TO COME

NO ONE KNOWS WHAT THE FUTURE HOLDS YET IN AS MUCH AS ONE
CAN EXPRESS

HAPPY FIRST ANNIVERSARY BABY FROM THE BOTTOM OF MY HEART

YOU ARE LOVED AND YOU ARE CARED FOR DEEPLY

TRUSTING

SHE HAS BEEN THINKING ABOUT THE RELATIONSHIP A LOT AS OF LATE AND SHE WONDERS IF SOMETHING WERE TO HAPPEN (NOT THAT SHE WISHES ANY BAD ON HIS REALTIONSHIP)

WOULD THEY WORK AS COUPLE BUILDING A LIFE TOGETHER?

WOULD HE WOULD CHEAT ON HER?

WOULD SHE BE ENOUGH FOR HIM? TO HEAR HIM SAY, "HE DOES NOT KNOW" MAKES HER WONDER WHY IS NO TRUST? THERE IS NO WAY TO MOVE FORWARD. IF SHE CAN NOT TRUST HIM THAT IS GOING TO BECOME A PROBLEM FOR THEM. .

TRUST IS SOMETHING THAT YOU CAN NOT GET BACK ONCE IT IS GONE OR HAS BEEN SEVERED. ALTHOUGH IT WAS NEVER HER INTENTION TO FEEL AS IF SHE COULD NOT TRUST THIM AT TIMES BUT HIS SNEAKY AND DECEPTIVE WAYS IS THE VERY REASON THAT IS A REALITY. SHE DOES NOT EXPECT TO HEAR FROM HIM AGAIN BECAUSE SHE HAS TO BE CONTENT AND BE ABLE TO TRUST HIM TO BE WITH HIM. WE GAVE IT A CHANCE. THE ACTIONS OF A PERSON OR THE PRECEIVED ACTIONS MAKES HER FEEL AS IF SHE CAN NOT TRUST HIM. THIS IS ALWAYS GOING TO BE A CONCERN ESPECIALLY WHEN SHE KNOWS THAT WHAT SHE IS DOING WITH HIM HAS TRUST ISSUES ALL OVER IT.

SHE WILL ALWAYS CARE FOR HIM AND SHE IS VERY GREATFUL FOR THE TIME THAT THEY DID SHARE. THERE ARE GOOD PEOPLE IN THIS WORLD AND SHE PRAYS THAT THEY EACH FIND THAT ONE PERSON THAT WILL BE THERE AND LOVE THEM AND THEY ARE ABLE TO TRUST.

THINKING OF YOU

(THIS IS WHAT I HAVE IMAGINED)

THINKING OF YOU

THE MAN THAT I WILL BE WITH AN ETERNITY

YOU ARE SMART HANDSOME AND YOU ARE TRUE

OR ARE YOU HERE TO MAKE ME BLUE JUST KNOW THAT I AM THINKING OF YOU

THINKING OF YOU

I AM FOND OF YOU AND I HOPE AND PRAY

THAT YOU FEEL THE SAME WAY

CARING AND SHARING LOVING EACH OTHER THE REST OF OUR DAYS

OUR LOVE WILL LAST AND BE ALWAYS

THINKING OF YOU

WHAT YOU LIKE TO DO YOUR FAVORITE SONG

MANY THOUGHTS OF YOU THROUGHOUT THE DAY LONG

THINKING OF YOU

WHEN I SEE YOU I SHINE LIKE A LIGHT

THAT IS SUCH A GOOD FEELING IT JUST FEELS RIGHT

THINKING OF YOU

THE FEELING THAT I HAVE ARE NEW

I CAN NOT REMEMBER WHEN I HAVE FELT LIKE THIS I HAVE NOT A CLUE

THINKING OF YOU

CAN IT BE THAT YOU ARE THE ONLY MAN FOR ME

THE ONLY FACE THAT I WILL BE PLEASED TO SEE

THE MAN THAT I CALL MY KING

PLEASING EACH OTHER IN EVERYTHING

UNCERTAIN

YOU WAKE UP WITH A STRANGE FEELING IN THE PIT OF YOUR
STOMACH THAT SOMETHING IS NOT RIGHT

UNCERTAIN

YOU GO THROUGHOUT THE DAY TRYING TO DO WHAT SEEMS NORMAL
AND DISMISS THE UNSETTLED FEELING THAT STILL EXISTS

UNCERTAIN

YOU COMMUNICATE YET SOMEHOW THE TONE IS DIFFERENT

IT IS NOT THE SAME

ARE YOU IMAGINING THIS

UNCERTAIN

YOU MAKE EXCUSES FOR THIS AND THAT

THEN YOU START TO QUESTION YOURSELF

DID YOU DO SOMETHING

WAS IT SOMETHING THAT YOU SAID

IS HE HAVING SECOND THOUGHTS

WHAT IS GOING ON INSIDE OF HIS HEAD

UNCERTAIN

YOU KNOW FROM THE BOTTOMLESS FEELING INSIDE THAT THINGS CAN
NOT GO ON LIKE THIS

UNCERTAIN

DO YOU SAY HOW YOU FEEL OR DO YOU DO WHAT YOU FEEL IS
INEVITABLE

UNCERTAIN

THINGS CAN NOT CONTINUE TO GO ON THIS WAY

YOU REALIZE THAT THERE IS SOMETHING THAT IS TROUBLING YOU BUT YOU CAN NOT SEEM TO GET THE RESOLUTION THAT IS MOST WANTED

UNCERTAIN

THERE IS A PART OF YOU THAT WILL CHERISH ALL THE TIMES TOGETHER BOTH GOOD AND BAD

UNCERTAIN

ON THE OTHER HAND YOU KNOW THAT IT IS TIME TO MOVE ON

ONCE YOU ARE ACCUSTOMED TO A PERSON PLACE OR THING IT CAN BE HARD TOO DIFFICULT TO LET IT GO ALTHOUGH YOU KNOW THAT PERSON PLACE OR THING IS NOT THE BEST FOR YOU

UNCERTAIN

YOU ARE HOLDING ON TO A FANTASY OF SOMETHING THAT HAS TO END

REALISTICALLY YOU KNOW OR YOU KNEW THAT THIS DAY WOULD COME BUT PROLONGING IT DID NOT OR IS NOT HELPING OR GOOD FOR ANYONE

UNCERTAIN

IT HAS BECOME VERY CERTAIN AT THIS POINT AND NOW YOU MUST DO WHAT IS NEEDED

GO ON WITH YOUR LIFE

LET GO IT IS TIME TO HURT FOR A WHILE BUT KNOW IT DOES NOT LAST

THE PAIN WILL NOT LAST

UNCERTAIN

ONCE YOU TOTALLY LET GO AND GET A GRIP ON THE KNOWLEDGE IT IS
BETTER TO BE WITHOUT A PERSON PLACE OR THING AND CONTENT
THAN TO BE WITH A PERSON PLACE OR THING AND MISERABLE

UNHAPPY WOMAN

UNHAPPY WOMAN

WHY DO YOU SAY THAT YOU ARE UNHAPPY

IS IT BECAUSE YOU FEEL CRAPPY

UNHAPPY WOMAN

YOU HAVE A LOT GOING FOR YOU

DO NOT STAY BLUE

UNHAPPY WOMAN

ARE YOU A VICTIM OF CIRCUMSTANCE

BE OPEN TO TAKING A CHANCE

UNHAPPY WOMAN

PUT ON A SMILE AND THINK ON THIS

THERE IS NO REASON THAT YOU SHOULD NOT HAVE BLISS

UNHAPPY WOMAN

YOU ARE STRONG

STATE WHAT IS WRONG

UNHAPPY WOMAN

I BELIEVE IN YOU AND KNOW THAT YOU CAN

UNHAPPY WOMAN

THINK OF THE WATER AND THE SAND AND KNOW THAT EVERYTHING

WILL BE

COULD BE

SHALL BE

GRAND

UNHAPPY WOMAN

ONCE YOU REALIZE THAT YOU WILL NO LONGER BE AN UNHAPPY WOMAN

BUT A WOMAN THAT IS FOCUSED, DRIVEN AND WORKING TOWARDS HER PLAN

WHEN I AM TOSSED AND DRIVEN

WHEN I AM TOSSED AND DRIVEN LIKE THE WIND

A CALM WORD YOU SEND

WHEN I AM TOSSED AND DRIVEN

THERE ARE DAYS WHEN I WANT TO BEND

YOU DO NOT REMIND ME OF MY BEGINNING YOU REMIND ME OF MY END

WHEN I AM TOSSED AND DRIVEN

I CAN NOT SEEM TO DO WHAT IS RIGHT

YOU LET ME KNOW THAT I AM IN YOUR SIGHT

WHEN I AM TOSSED AND DRIVEN

I LOOK FOR A PLACE TO GET MY SELF TOGETHER

YOU SAY COME TO ME YOUR PROBLEMS ARE LIGHT AS A FEATHER

WHEN I AM TOSSED AND DRIVEN

I HAVE GOTTEN OFF TASK

YOU ARE THERE AND THERE IS NO MASK

WHEN I AM TOSSED AND DRIVEN

I WANT TO SEE ME AS YOU DO WITHOUT A SPOT OR FLAW

YOU REMIND ME THAT I AM THE APPLE OF YOUR EYE AND THAT IS ALL YOU SAW

WHEN I AM TOSSED AND DRIVEN

YOU ARE THERE YOU HAVE ALWAYS BEEN THERE FOR ME

YOU HAVE NOT CAST ME INTO THE SEA

WHEN I AM TOSSED AND DRIVEN

I RUN TO YOU AND WANT YOU TO OPEN YOUR ARMS AND HOLD ME

AT THAT POINT THERE IS NO OTHER PLACE THAT I WOULD RATHER BE

WORDS CAN NOT EXPRESS

WORDS CAN NOT EXPRESS HOW I FEEL ABOUT YOU BUT I WILL TRY

THESE THREE YEARS HAVE HAD UPS, DOWNS AND GREAT TIMES WITH SO MANY LOVING MEMORIES

I CONSIDER YOU TO BE MY MAN AND I AM YOUR WOMAN ALTHOUGH IN REALITY WE BOTH KNOW WE HAVE NO IDEA WHERE THIS WILL GO

I WANT YOU TO KNOW THAT I HAVE GIVEN YOU MY HEART, BODY, AND ALL THAT COMES WITH THAT AND I AM LOVING YOU MORE THAN I COULD HAVE IMAGINED

WHEN WE ARE TOGETHER BABY THINGS JUST FEEL SO RIGHT AND WHEN WE ARE APART I FEEL AS IF A PART OF ME IS MISSING

WE DID NOT PLAN OR EXPECT TO BE TOGETHER BABY BUT I AM SO GLAD THAT YOU DID NOT GIVE UP ON US

I REALIZE THAT YOU DO NOT LIKE A LOT OF WORDS SO I WILL BE AS BRIEF AS I CAN

YOU ARE MY DREAM COME TRUE AND I AM SO HAPPY WITH YOU IN MY LIFE

TOGETHER WE ARE A DYNAMIC DUO AND THERE IS NOT ANYTHING THAT WE CAN NOT DO. I WILL ALWAYS LOVE AND CHERISH WHAT WE HAVE

I WANT TO HAVE MANY MORE WORDS THAT CAN NOT EXPRESS TOGETHER WITH YOU

WRITING ON THE WALL

TAKE HEED TO THE WRITING ON THE WALL

WHEN THE WRITING IS CLEAR AND THE SIGNS SEEM TO VALIDATE

WHY NOT PAY ATTENTION

LEST YOU FALL

TAKE HEED TO THE WRITING ON THE WALL

FOOLISH LADY OF MINE ALL THE ARROWS POINT TO STAY AWAY
PROCEED WITH CAUTION GO THE OTHER WAY AND DO NOT TOUCH

LEST YOU FALL

TAKE HEED TO THE WRITING ON THE WALL

THE SIGNS ARE DOUBLED THAT MEANS TWICE THE TROUBLE YET YOU
DON'T SEEM TO PAY ATTENTION AND GOVERN YOURSELF
ACCORDINGLY

LEST YOU FALL

TAKE HEED TO THE WRITING ON THE WALL

FOOLISH LADY OF MINE WHY NOW DO YOU DECIDE TO IGNORE THE
WRITING ON THE WALL

LEST YOU FALL

TAKE HEED TO THE WRITING ON THE WALL

FOOLISH LADY OF MINE YOU ARE TO BE WISER, SMARTER, READY TO
CUT OFF THE CHOAS BEFORE IT STARTS NIP IT IN THE BUD

LEST YOU FALL

TAKE HEED TO THE WRITING ON THE WALL

FOOLISH LADY OF MINE YOU DISAPPOINT WITH THE THROW CAUTION TO THE WIND MIND SET WHEN YOU HAVE BEEN SO CAREFUL NOT TO MAKE WAVES AND PAY CLOSE ATTENTION TO THE WRITING ON THE WALL

LEST YOU FALL

TAKE HEED TO THE WRITING ON THE WALL

PICK YOURSELF UP DO NOT STAY DOWN IT HAPPENS NOW FOOLISH LADY OF MINE YOU CAN TURN THIS AROUND DUST YOURSELF OFF AND GET ON COURSE

LEST YOU FALL

TAKE HEED TO THE WRITING ON THE WALL

YOU ARE NO LONGER THE FOOLISH LADY OF MINE YOU FOUND YOUR DIRECTION AND ARE WORKING TOWARDS THE WISE LADY YOU HAVE BEEN BEFORE

LEST YOU FALL

TAKE HEED TO THE WRITING ON THE WALL

WISE LADY OF MINE YOU TOOK THE WRONG PATH AND LOST SIGHT OF THE COURSE FOR JUST A WHILE BUT NOW YOU ARE THRIVING AND MOVING FORWARD IT IS OKAY TO GET OFF COURSE AND LEARN THAT THE WRITING ON THE WALL IS A GUIDE AND IS THERE TO HELP ALONG THE WAY

LEST YOU FALL

TAKE HEED TO THE WRITING ON THE WALL

WISE LADY OF MINE TAKE COMFORT IN KNOWING THAT YOU ARE NOT THE FIRST TO STRAY FROM THE WRITING ON THE WALL BE HAPPY IN THE FACT THAT YOU REALIZED BEFORE IT WAS TOO LATE THAT THE DIRECTION YOU WERE TAKING WAS NOT FOR YOU

LEST YOU FALL

WOMAN OF EXCELLENCE

A WOMAN OF EXCELLENCE IS A MATURE ADULT HUMAN FEMALE

THAT IS EQUIPPED TO SOAR AND MAINTAIN NOT TRAIL

A WOMAN OF EXCELLENCE IS A PERSON WHO HAS FEMININE QUALITIES

SOMEONE WHO KNOWS HOW TO CONDUCT HERSELF FULL OF
KNOWLWDGE AND SEES

A WOMAN OF EXCELLENCE IS A WOMAN OF QUALITY AND A SENSE OF
BEING SUPERIOR

THERE IS NO TIME FOR FEELING INFERIOR

OUTSTANDING IS HOW YOU ARE PERCEIVED

NOT HAUGHTY OR EASILY DECEIVED

A WOMAN OF EXCELLENCE IS OF THE HIGHEST GRADE

YET ABIDING IN THE SECRET PLACE OF THE MOST HIGH WILL BE YOUR
SHADE

GOD CREATED YOU TO BE WISE, SMART, LOVING AND BOLD

GOD IS ALWAYS THERE WHEN YOU NEED A HAND TO HOLD

A WOMAN OF EXCELLENCE WILL ALWAYS REMEMBER THAT YOU ARE
FEARFULLY AND WONDERFULLY MADE

YOU ARE MORE PRECIOUS THAN JADE

YOU ARE ALL THAT I WANT

YOU ARE ALL THAT I WANT

WHEN WE FIRST MET I HAD DECIDED THAT WE WOULD NOT BE MORE
THAN FRIENDS

THAT IS NOT HOW THIS ENDS

YOU ARE ALL THAT I WANT

YOU MADE ME LAUGH AND THEN I KNEW

MY THOUGHTS OF YOU GREW

YOU ARE ALL THAT I WANT

WHEN I WENT OUT WITH YOU

I FELT A CONNECTION SOMETHING NEW

YOU ARE ALL THAT I WANT

I FELT WEAK IN MY KNEES AND I WAS ON A HOOK

I HAD TO TAKE A SECOND LOOK

YOU ARE ALL THAT I WANT

I TRIED TO RESIST AND SAY THAT THIS COULD NEVER BE

BUT I COULD SEE

THAT YOU WERE ALL I WANTED FOR ME

YOU ARE ALL THAT I WANT

HOW COULD THIS BE I WANTED TO SEE YOU SPEAK WITH YOU

IS IT POSSBLE YOU WANT ME TOO

YOU ARE ALL THAT I WANT

I HAVE BEEN THINKING OF YOU

AND YOU HAVE CALLED OR TEXTED ME TOO

YOU ARE ALL THAT I WANT

I CAN BE DIFFICULT AND I WANT MY WAY

THAT COULD BE A REASON FOR YOU NOT TO STAY

YOU ARE ALL I WANT

I HAVE TRIED MY BEST TO KEEP MY FEELINGS AT BAY

I WAS NOT SURE IF YOU FELT THE SAME WAY

YOU ARE ALL THAT I WANT

I REALIZE THAT THERE ARE THINGS I CAN NOT MODIFY

I ALSO KNOW THAT I CAN NOT LIE

YOU ARE ALL THAT I WANT

I SIT ALONE AND THINK ABOUT THE GOOD TIMES GOOD BYE

BUT IT IS NOT THAT EASY TO BE WITHOUT YOU YET I TRY

YOU ARE ALL THAT I WANT

HOW COULD THINGS THAT ARE SO PERFECT BETWEEN US

WHEN YOU ARE ALL THAT I WANT

I COULD SEE YOU BY MY SIDE

YOU ARE ALL THAT I WANT

I THINK OF YOU DAY AND NIGHT

I FEEL WITH CERTAINTY THAT THIS IS RIGHT

YOU ARE ALL THAT I WANT

YOU ARE ALL THAT I WISH FOR

I CAN NOT DESIRE ANY MORE

YOU ARE ALL THAT I WANT

WHEN WE ARE RUNNING ERRANDS AND SHARED MOMENTS

IT IS VALUED TIME SPENT

YOU ARE ALL THAT I WANT

YOU HAVE BEEN HONEST WITH ME

NOW THAT MY EYES ARE OPEN I CAN SEE

YOU ARE ALL THAT I WANT

SOME THINGS ARE NOT MEANT TO BE

SO I HAVE SET YOU FREE

WE COULD NEVER BE

YOU ARE ALL THAT I WANT

NO MATTER HOW MUCH WE MAY WANT THIS TO BE

THE THINGS THAT YOU HAVE GOING ON WILL NOT ALLOW US TO BE

YOU ARE ALL THAT I WANT

I WANT YOU TO BE HAPPY

EVEN IF THAT IS NOT WITH ME

YOU ARE ALL THAT I WANT

I COULD HAVE DONE THIS IN A BETTER MANNER

I AM HURTING AND IT SHOWS LIKE A BANNER

YOU ARE ALL THAT I WANT

MY FEELINGS FOR YOU ARE TRUE

I HAVE NEVER FELT LIKE THIS BEFORE

AND ALL I WANT IS YOU

YOU ARE RIGHT

YOU ARE RIGHT WHEN YOU SAID THAT YOU CAN NOT GIVE HER WHAT SHE WANTS. ALL SHE WANTED WAS TO ADD TO EACH OTHERS HAPPINESS AND BUILD SOMETHING TOGETHER. SHER GAVE YOU HER ALL, HER BEST AND SHE LOVED YOU WITH ALL OF HER HEART. THE FACT IS YOU USED TO BE ALL SHE WANTED AND YOU WOULD HAVE BEEN ENOUGH FOR HER BUT SHE WOULD NEVER BE ALL THAT YOU WANTED.

SHE IS NOT ANGRY WITH YOU HOWEVER, JUST SICK AND TIRED OF BEING SICK AND TIRED. YOU WILL NEVER BE THE MAN FOR HER SHE HAS REACHED THAT RESOLVE IN HER LIFE BECAUSE SHE NEEDED SOMEONE THAT IS NOT MARRIED AND THAT DOES NOT HAVE SOMEONE ELSE IN HIS LIFE THAT HE HAS FEELINGS FOR AND HAS TO PAY HER PHONE BILL IN ORDER TO MAINTAIN A CONSTANT COMMITMENT WITH HER.

SHE NEEDED SOMEONE THAT IS NOT DECEPTIVE AND CRAFTY WHERE THIS PERSON IS CONCERNED LEAVING THE ROOM TO MAKE SECRET PHONE CALLS OR CODED TEXTS. MAKING SURE THAT WHAT EVER SHE NEEDS OR WANTS IS PURCHASED. OUR TIME WILL NEVER BE OUR TIME BECAUSE THE WIFE OR THE PERSON YOU ARE COMMITTED TO WILL CALL AND EVERY CALL WILL BE ANSWERED NO MATTER HOW SHE FELT. HER FEELINGS DO NOT MATTER THEY NEVER HAVE AND THEY NEVER WILL. THEY ARE JUST THAT HER FEELINGS. WHY SHOULD THEY MATTER WHEN YOU ARE GETTING EVERYTHING THAT YOU WANT?

SHE NEEDED SOMEONE THAT WANTS HER AND NOT THIS ONE AND THAT. SAYING THAT SHE IS THE ONLY ONE YOU ARE BEING INTIMATE WITH WHEN CLEARLY PICTURES IN YOUR PHONE ARE TO THE CONTRARYAND MAKES IT VERY DIFFICULT FOR HER TO BELIEVE.

KNOWING THAT WORDS ARE JUST WORDS I LOVE YOU, I WANT YOU AND I WANT TO DO SOMETHING FOR YOU BUT IT NEVER WORKS OUT YET WHERE OTHERS ARE INVOLVED THERE IS NEVER A BEAT MISSED. WHATEVER AND WHENEVER A CALL IS MADE IT IS ANSWERED,

WHENEVER A RIDE IS NEEDED, WHENEVER SOMETHING NEEDS TO BE GIVEN OR PURCHASED THAT PLAN ALWAYS MANIFESTS YET IT NEVER SEEMS TO WORK OUT FOR HER ACCOUNT BECAUSE SHE NEVER WAS AND NEVER WILL BE THE PRIORITY IN YOUR LIFE BUT IT'S OBVIOUS WHO IS.

SHE WANTED SOMEONE THAT WANTS TO REMEMBER HER BIRTHDAY (NOT JUST EVERY PERSON THAT HE HAS BEEN WITH IN THE PAST AND CURRENTLY) YET DOES NOT SEEM TO CARE ENOUGH TO JUST ACKNOWLEDGE HERS AND SHE WANTED SOMEONE THAT WANTS TO CELEBRATE THE DATE THEY BECAME OFFICAL.

YOUR LIFE IS PROGRESSING FORWARD AS IT ALWAYS WILL AND A MAN THAT HAS EVERYTHING BUT A BENZ AND JET IS VERY FORTUNATE.

YOU ARE FREE

I HAVE BEEN THINKING AND I WANT YOU TO KNOW THAT FOR THE LIFE OF ME I CAN NOT UNDERSTAND WHY YOU CALLED ME AFTER TWO WEEKS. YOU WERE ALWAYS FREE TO DO WHAT YOU WANTED. GO OR COME WITH WHOMEVER YOU WANTED WITHOUT HEARING ONE THING FROM ME.

I WILL NEVER DO RIGHT I DO NOT KNOW HOW (THIS COMING FROM A MAN WHO DOES NOT KNOW THE MEANING OF RIGHT) I HAVE TRIED TO LOVE YOU AND TREAT YOU LIKE THE KING THAT I KNOW YOU ARE. I HAVE GIVEN MY BEST AND IT WILL NEVER BE ENOUGH. WE WILL NOT SEE ALL THINGS A LIKE AND I CAN NOT SAY WHAT WILL HAPPEN WHEN THAT DAY COMES.

YOU GAVE ME A CHOICE AND I AM LEAVING IT. I NO LONGER WANT TO TRY AND DEAL WITH BEING THE THIRD LEG IN YOUR LIFE. YOU DO WELL WITHOUT ME SO CONTINUE TO DO SO.

I WANT TO BE IN A NORMAL RELATIONSHIP BUT I DO NOT HAVE ANY IDEA WHAT THAT MEANS. YOU HAVE BEEN THE CLOSEST I WILL EVER HAVE TO A REALTIONSHIP AND YOU SEEM TO FEEL THAT I AM NOT DOING RIGHT BY YOU. YOU MAKE IT SEEM SO EASY BREEZY.

YOU HAVE CAPTURED MY HEART

YOU HAVE CAPTURED MY HEART MY SOUL AND ALL OF ME. WHO WOULD HAVE EVER IMAGINED THAT JUNE AND DECEMBER WOULD MAKE THE PERFECT COMBINATION? IN KEEPING WITH THE SPIRIT OF HONESTY I MUST SAY THAT AT TIMES I DO NOT KNOW WHY YOU STUCK IN HERE WITH ME ALL THIS TIME. I REALIZE THAT THIS JOURNEY HAS NOT BEEN ALL ROSES NEVERTHELESS HERE WE ARE DEFEATING ALL ODDS.

MY HEART BELONGS TO YOU MY SOUL BELONGS TO YOU MY BODY BELONGS TO YOU ALL THAT I AM AND ALL THAT I HOPE TO BE I WANT YOU WITH ME THROUGH IT ALL GOOD BAD HAPPY SAD. YOU MAY NOT HAVE SIGNED UP FOR THE LONG HAUL BUT WHEN I AM DREAMING OF YOU AND I YOU NEVER WANT TO LET ME GO AND IT MAKES ME WANT TO DO ALL THAT I CAN ONCE I HAVE AWOKE TO BE ALL THAT I CAN FOR YOU AND I.

YOU SAY THAT I CAN BE STUBBORN AND I SAY I AM STRONG WILLED BUT THE TRUTH OF THE MATTER YOU ARE THE GLUE THAT HOLDS US TOGETHER. I SMILE FOR WHAT APPEARS NO REASON BUT IT IS BECAUSE OF YOU. I CAN NOW LIVE MY LIFE TO THE FULLEST AND THAT IS BECAUSE OF YOU. YOU SAY THAT I ASSUME THINGS THAT ARE NOT THERE AND OF COURSE I BEG TO DIFFER.

THIS IS WHAT I KNOW:

EVERY SINCE WE HAVE BEEN TOGETHER YOU HAVE BROUGHT OUT THINGS I DID NOT KNOW EXSISTED IN ME. I LAUGH, I CRY, I LOVE, I EXPRESS MYSELF TO YOU LIKE NEVER BEFORE YOU ARE MY ONE TRUE LOVE. I HAVE BEEN IN WHAT I THOUGHT WAS LOVE BUT UNTIL THE FAITHFUL DAY IN MARCH FOUR YEARS AGO I DID NOT HAVE A CLUE.

HOW COULD ONE PERSON MAKE SUCH AN IMPACT IN MY LIFE FOR THE BETTER AND YET THERE ARE DAYS WHEN I FEEL LIKE THIS JUST CAN NOT BE RIGHT. HOW COULD LOVING YOU COME SO EASILY SO EFFORTLESSLY? IT IS BECAUSE WHEN IT IS RIGHT IT IS RIGHT. I FEEL

THAT THIS IS RIGHT AND WE ARE GREAT TOGETHER AND APART SHOULD NOT BE. WE ARE FROM TWO DIFFERENT WORLDS IT WOULD APPEAR BUT TOGETHER WE ARE IN PERFECT RHYTHM NOT SKIPPING A BEAT. I HOPE THAT IN TIME TO COME YOU WILL LOOK BACK AND REFLECT ON THESE WORDS AND THEY SOMEHOW MAKE YOU FEEL SPECIAL AND LOVED. WHEN I WAKE AND YOU ARE ON MY MIND I DO NOT WANT IT ANY OTHER WAY. WHEN I AM THINKING OF YOU AND YOU CALL OR TEXT SOMEHOW I FEEL YOU ARE THINKING OF ME. LOVE AND TRUST CAN NOT BE PAID FOR BUT IT IS EARNED AND YOU HAVE UNLIMITED STOCK IN ME. WORDS CAN NOT REALLY EXPRESS HOW I REALLY FEEL AND SOMETIMES NEITHER DO MY ACTIONS BUT DEEP DOWN I HOPE AND PRAY THAT YOU HAVE SOME IDEA

I WOULD LIKE TO SAY THAT MOVING FORWARD WILL BE A PIECE OF CAKE BUT WHAT I CAN EXPRESS IS THAT I WANT IT TO BE WITH YOU. I DO NOT KNOW WHAT THE FUTURE HOLDS FOR YOU AND ME YET I WILL ANXIOUSLY WAIT WHAT IS TO COME. I WOULD LIKE TO IMAGINE THAT ONE DAY WE WOULD WISK OFF TO PLACES UNKNOWN AND SAY I DO BUT WISHFUL THINKING WON'T MAKE IT COME TRUE. I SUPPOSE I WOULD SETTLE WITH STAYING ON TRACK WITH EACH OTHER FOR THE REST OF DAYS.

I WILL ALWAYS LOVE AND CHERISH OUR TIME TOGETHER FOR ALL OF MY DAYS

THE MAN IN MY DREAMS

THERE IS NOT GOING TO BE

THERE IS NOT GOING TO BE

DAYS WHEN WE LOOK INTO EACH OTHERS EYES UNTIL WE GET LOST AND HOLD EACH OTHERS HAND

AT LEAST NOT WITH ME

THERE IS NOT GOING TO BE

A TIME WHEN WE WALK AMONG THE STARS OR WALK IN THE SAND

AT LEAST NOT WITH ME

THERE IS NOT GOING TO BE

TIMES WHEN WE SPEND ROMATIC DINNERS AND DANCING

AT LEAST NOT WITH ME

THERE IS NOT GOING TO BE

DAYS WHEN WE STAY IN AT OUR LEISURE AND SNUGGLE AND FEED EACH OTHER UNTIL WE HAVE HAD ENOUGH

AT LEAST NOT WITH ME

THERE IS NOT GOING TO BE

ANY HOLIDAYS, BIRTHDAYS, ANNIVERSARIES, JUST BECAUSE DAYS THAT WE SPEND TOGETHER

AT LEAST NOT WITH ME

THERE IS NOT GOING TO BE

BEING THERE FOR EACH OTHER THRU THICK AND THIN HAPPY AND SAD GOOD AND BAD

AT LEAST NOT WITH ME

THERE IS NOT GOING TO BE

A TIME WHEN WE KISS EACH OTHER PASSIONATELY

AT LEAST NOT WITH ME

THERE IS NOT GOING TO BE

TIMES WHEN WE EMBRACE AND ARE INTIMATE FROM SUN UP UNTIL
SUN DOWN

AT LEAST NOT WITH ME

THERE IS NOT GOING TO BE

I LOVE YOU AND I AM GLAD THAT WE COMPLETE EACH OTHER AND
YOU ARE THE ONLY ONE FOR ME

AT LEAST NOT WITH ME

IS THIS LOVE

WHEN YOU CAN'T SEEM TO TEAR YOURSELF AWAY FROM THIS PERSON

IS THIS LOVE

WHEN YOU ARE SPEAKING WITH THEM AND ALL YOU WANT TO DO IS
BE IN THEIR PRESENCE

IS THIS LOVE

WHEN YOU ARE AWAY FROM EACH OTHER ALL YOU DO IS TRY TO
THINK OF WAYS TO BE WHERE THE PERSON IS

IS THIS LOVE

WHEN THERE IS A YEARNING DEEP INSIDE TO HAVE ANY CONTACT OF
ANY KIND WITH THE PERSON

IS THIS LOVE

WHEN YOU SIT AND THINK OF THINGS THAT THE PERSON SAID AND
YOU SMILE AND LAUGH TO YOURSELF

IS THIS LOVE

WHEN YOU WANT TO KNOW WHAT THE PERSON IS DOING AND THE
PERSON CONTACTS YOU

IS THIS LOVE

WHEN YOU LOOK AT GIFTS AND CARDS THAT YOU HAVE RECEIVED
FROM THE PERSON AND TEARS STREAM

IS THIS LOVE

WHEN YOU FEEL LIKE WHEN YOU ARE APART A PIECE OF YOU IS
MISSING

IS THIS LOVE

WHEN YOU GET LOST LOOKING INTO THE EYES OF THE PERSON

IS THIS LOVE

WHEN YOU ARE IN THE ARMS OF THE PERSON AND YOU CAN NOT OR DO NOT WANT TO LET GO

IS THIS LOVE

WHEN YOU CAN SEE FOREVER BRIGHTER THAN YOU HAD IMAGINED BECAUSE OF THE PERSON

IS THIS LOVE

I LOVE YOU LORD

I NOW KNOW YOUR LOVE IS TRUE

EVEN IF I DO NOT KNOW WHAT TO SAY OR WHAT TO DO

I LOVE YOU LORD

I DO NOT LOOK TO MY LEFT OR MY RIGHT

I FOCUS ON YOU AND KEEP YOU IN MY SIGHT

I LOVE YOU LORD

NO MATTER WHAT IS GOING ON

I HAVE YOU TO LEAN AND DEPEND ON

I LOVE YOU LORD

I CAST ALL MY CARES ON YOU

BECAUSE THAT IS THE BEST THING FOR ME TO DO

I LOVE YOU LORD

OH I CAN TRY TO MAKE IT FIT OR MAKE IT RIGHT

I HAVE TO REMEMBER IT IS NOT MY FIGHT

I LOVE YOU LORD

LONGING FOR YOUR HAND TO HOLD

IS NEVER WRONG THAT IS WHAT I HAVE BEEN TOLD

ON THAT BELIEF I AM SOLD

KNOWING THAT IS BETTER THAN ANY AMOUNT OF GOLD

I LOVE YOU LORD

I LOVE YOU I REALLY DO

EVEN WHEN I AM SAD I REALLY DO I REALLY DO

www.ingramcontent.com/pod-product-compliance
Lightning Source LLC
Chambersburg PA
CBHW071418040426
42445CB00012BA/1202